AFFIRMING

AFFIRMING

A Memoir of Faith, Sexuality, and Staying in the Church

SALLY GARY

William B. Eerdmans Publishing Company
Grand Rapids, Michigan

Wm. B. Eerdmans Publishing Co.
4035 Park East Court SE, Grand Rapids, Michigan 49546
www.eerdmans.com

Published 2021
Printed in the United States of America

27 26 25 24 23 22 21   1 2 3 4 5 6 7

ISBN 978-0-8028-7917-2

Library of Congress Cataloging-in-Publication Data

A catalog record for this book is available from the Library of Congress.

Unless otherwise noted, Scripture quotations come from the New International Version (2011).

For my mama, who introduced me to Jesus

Contents

Acknowledgments

The older I become, the more I realize that we accomplish nothing on our own. We achieve only on the shoulders of others. That's the essence of this book – how others have influenced my thinking and helped to bring me to where I am today. Most of all, I thank my parents for their ongoing influence in my life. I'm thankful for all those Sunday school teachers and public school teachers who planted, tilled, and watered seeds along the way. I'm thankful for those professors who shaped and refined me, and for the friends who educated me in all my academic endeavors. And to all those who are not specifically named in this memoir but who most assuredly impacted my faith and the process by which I came to be affirming, thank you. You are all dear to me.

Thank you to all those who have walked on the journey with me. Would that I had known years ago what I know now. How different our lives might have been. For all of the pain my lack of awareness may have caused, I am deeply sorry. Likewise, not everyone will be pleased with the words on the pages of this book. I ask for your grace and understanding, as I continue to offer mine. This is not the end of the conversation. Rather, it is a new beginning.

In 2013, Leafwood Press of Abilene Christian University took a great risk in publishing my memoir, *Loves God, Likes Girls*. The message of the book was greatly needed among its conservative readership, requiring tremendous courage for Leonard Allen, director of Leafwood at the time, to print. While my views have since shifted, the good that was accomplished through that memoir will never be forgotten. Thank you, Leonard, for your wisdom in opening a door that was unprecedented, and for starting conversations that were long overdue and, I pray, ongoing in our churches. Thank you also to Jason Fikes, current director of Leafwood, for your continued interest and support.

I am especially grateful for all the pioneers in the Christian LGBTQ movement, but especially for the voices of Justin Lee and Matthew Vines. Justin and Matthew have led the way in awakening fellow believers to the wrestlings of Christian LGBTQ people. I am indebted to their courage and the time and energy expended in ministering to the LGBTQ community and to the church. I'm thankful for their friendship and for their willingness to "go first," making it all that much easier for me to write this book.

Without human cattle prods who kept this book alive in me, I would not have been self-disciplined enough to finish. John Alan Turner, thank you for remembering that I'm "Seabiscuit," the champion racehorse – capable of greatness and yet often content to loll around in bluegrass and nap in the sunshine – and still believing in me. Thank you, my friend, for continuing to talk to me about writing when others had given up. Thanks for inviting me to the writers retreat with you and the Runkels. That weekend in Seattle with all of you was a huge turning point in the completion of this book.

Thank you to those who have graciously allowed me to tell parts of their stories, because their stories overlapped with mine. Now I can no longer share my story completely without telling some of theirs as well.

Thank you to the readers of early drafts – Pat Bills, Mike Cope, Nancy Ulrich, and Gil Vollmering. I am grateful for your abiding friendship, and for the combination of candor and grace you demonstrate with me. Rare are those friends who will be honest, holding my feet to the fire, yet reassuring and kind. I am becoming a better person because of you.

Trevor Thompson, thank you for a conversation long ago that was a huge turning point for my faith. I will always be grateful. More recently, I am so appreciative of this opportunity to work with you, Laurel Draper, Tom Raabe, and the rest of the Eerdmans team. Thank you all for your sensitivity to this topic and for your desire to bring this book to life. For your willingness to be flexible in working with my schedule and the ministry needs of the CenterPeace "e3" Conference, I can't thank you enough.

Most of all, I thank Karen Keen for the hours you spent editing my stories. For all the hours of listening to my stories and ideas for yet another chapter. For having the wisdom and courage to say, "Less is more, Sally!" For believing in me and for praying for this book to open hearts to God. For encouraging me when all the time, you, Karen, are the real writer in our family! For warmth, comfort, security, and inspiration. For making home wherever you are. I love you.

Oh. And thank you to Rudy, the miniature dapple dachshund who slept by my side as I typed every word.

Author's Note

In writing this book I have relied primarily on my memory and, when able, the recollections of friends in the stories. Most of the names used in the book, but not all, have been changed for the sake of the privacy of those individuals. Sometimes certain details have been omitted or altered to protect anonymity. I have not created any composite characters for this book.

Prologue

In many ways it was a typical Sunday morning. I got up, showered, put on some clothes, and headed to church, as I'd been doing for as long as I could remember. But there was something different about this drive to church.

"God," I prayed. "I'm not completely sure about this. Sometimes the feelings I have for this woman – feelings that go much deeper than friendship – seem like a gift from you. The emotional, intellectual, and spiritual connection I feel with her is so much more than mere physical attraction, and yet that's a part of what I feel as well. I can't stop thinking about her. I want to be with her all the time. Our conversations about ministry and Scripture and the similarities in our backgrounds in church just keep drawing me closer to her. She's exactly what I've always wanted in a partner to share my life with, mainly because of how much she loves you."

I continued praying as I turned onto the highway to begin the drive to church. "But, God, at other times I feel like I'm violating something sacred, something I've been taught all my life is the vilest of sins. I don't know what you expect from me.

How do I determine whether what I'm experiencing with her is really from you . . . or not?"

I could feel the tension in my body, the shallow breathing, the elevated heart rate. I'd felt those physiological responses to emotional stress at different points throughout my life, so they weren't unfamiliar. This just felt bigger, more important to resolve.

I kept driving down the 635 loop around Dallas, inching my way over to the right lane to take the Jupiter exit, and, finally, I pulled into the church parking lot. Walking to the side door, I could hear the singing already under way, indicating I was running a bit late. I walked through the crowd, greeting people with hugs, searching for a seat. When I finally settled into my pew, I joined in singing with these people who had become family to me over the last several years. I placed membership with the Highland Oaks Church in 2014, when I moved from Abilene to Dallas to expand the ministry that I was doing with CenterPeace, a nonprofit organization I started in 2006 to equip churches, schools, and families to have more Christlike conversations on faith and sexuality.

Just as I had done almost every Sunday morning of my life, I participated in the regular rhythms of a Church of Christ service – prayer and singing, listening to the announcements, sharing the Lord's Supper, and absorbing the sermon. But on this particular Sunday morning, I experienced a deep angst in the pit of my stomach, reflecting my inner conflict. One that, on the surface, could only be resolved by either giving up a spiritual identity in the Church of Christ or giving up the woman who was becoming the love of my life.

My pastor, Pat, stepped onto the stage, Bible in hand, and walked toward the crowd. Smiling from ear to ear, his bright blue eyes twinkling, he greeted us enthusiastically with a warm "Morning, church!" Then he began his sermon. Being a singer, he often incorporated a song into the lesson, and that's what he did on this particular Sunday. The song was familiar and had played an incredibly meaningful role in my life more than twenty years earlier. The beginning lines are "Make me more free, free me. More free from my old life, more free in my new."[1] It goes on to ask God for the kind of freedom that allows us to love God more, to rise above sin into newness of life, and to keep our eyes ever on Jesus.

The first time I ever heard "Make Me More Free" was at a concert in a Baptist church in Houston. Dennis Jernigan, a popular Christian songwriter and worship leader in the 1990s, was well known for sharing his story at praise and worship nights he led across the country. Dennis revealed to the audience that he had wrestled with his sexuality all his life. He had been attracted to the same sex since a young age and tried desperately to reconcile his sexuality with his faith. His music grew out of a lot of pain and confusion, as well as a deep love for God.

I sat with rapt attention when Dennis began telling us about the song "Make Me More Free." It was connected to the story of Jesus raising Lazarus from the dead. "Lazarus would never be more alive than at the moment that Jesus called him to come out from the grave," Dennis explained. "But Lazarus continued to gain freedom as, one by one, the grave linens were removed." Dennis drew a comparison to our lives; we couldn't be more saved than we were at the very first moment in which we believed, but we grow in freedom from sin over time as Jesus continues to "removes the grave clothes." The "more free" we are from the grave clothes of sin, the more freedom we experience in Christ. Over a lifetime, if we follow Christ's leading, we're transformed more and more into his likeness. For Dennis, that meant choosing not to be in a same-sex relationship. He believed it would be sinful to do so, even though it felt natural to him to love another man.

Dennis's story and the analogy he drew with Lazarus's resurrection from the dead resonated deeply with me. I sat there frozen in my seat, conscious that any movement might give away my secret that I, too, struggled with my sexuality. Yet I also felt a sense of freedom that I'd never felt before. Never before had I heard anyone who was a Christian, let alone a worship leader, admit to being attracted to his own sex. Hearing Dennis's testimony was a game-changer for me. For the first time in my life, I felt less alone. The song "Make Me More Free" was my story too. Over the next several years, Dennis's music was a constant in my life, and this song in particular became an anthem of sorts.

I didn't come out to anyone until I was thirty-five years old. I grew up in the 1960s and '70s, and back then talking about sexuality was pretty taboo in my world. Talking about homosexuality was unheard of, unless it involved hateful condemnation or jokes. It wasn't until college that I came to the realization that the feelings I'd had for girls, at least since high school, were indicative of my being gay. But back then I wouldn't have said that. I wouldn't have used the word "gay" to describe myself. The word "gay" in the late 1970s and '80s, even into the '90s, in my conservative Christian world, had more to do with someone's sexual behavior than with their sexual orientation. If you said someone was gay in 1982, it was taken to mean that the person was promiscuous and was literally having sex with anyone available. At least in my Texas Bible Belt world, that's what it meant. And it certainly didn't describe me.

When I first consciously acknowledged to myself in college that what I felt for a girl who was my best friend went deeper than friendship, I was confused. On one hand, having someone in my life to care for so deeply felt really good – even though she had no idea at the time that my feelings were romantic in nature. Yet, I was also horrified, because in my conservative Bible Belt world, being attracted to your own sex was the worst possible thing. Surely this can't be me, I said to myself. This can't be true. I'm the good little Church of Christ girl, remember? The one who always knew her memory verse, who made the decision to be baptized before the other kids, the leader of the youth group. I took my faith so seriously that I wouldn't even dance at school dances, and alcohol didn't touch my lips until much later in life. How could someone like me be attracted to girls?

I grew up in a world with taboos on sexuality, especially homosexuality. I was steeped in shame and swore to myself that I would carry this secret to my grave. The stigma I learned in childhood regarding people who are gay burrowed deep below the surface. Now all those feelings of disgust applied to me, or so I reasoned. I was at my lowest in my thirties. Miserable and depressed, I almost hit bottom before I was willing to admit to another human being that I was attracted to women. I couldn't imagine actually uttering those words aloud, but that's how desperate I was. The plan of keeping all these feelings locked in my head had gone completely awry, and I was at my wit's end. No longer could I keep up this facade of having it all together on the outside while on the inside I grew increasingly lonely. I was miserable. Looking back on that time of my life, I can see very clearly that everything was coming to a head.

This is where I was when I attended Dennis's concert. I had never heard of anyone who had experienced a drastic change in sexual orientation before. I certainly didn't know anyone personally. Yet Dennis seemed to have changed. And at that time change is what was expected of all of us who experienced same-sex attraction. So, I trusted that if this is what God wanted for me, God would provide what I needed to make it happen. I just had to be open to whatever God wanted to do in my life. If that meant a change in the very natural desire I felt for women, then so be it. Did I believe that God could change someone's sexual orientation? Yes, I did.

Along with hearing Dennis Jernigan's testimony, I read a book called *Portraits of Freedom* that presented fourteen stories of men and women who had identified as gay or lesbian back in the 1980s but now professed change in their sexual orientation. Like many of us in the Christian LGBTQ community, I wanted so badly to believe that was possible. Believing in the possibility of change provided me with a sense of hope for my life. I had grown up believing my only options were to marry a man or remain single, so the idea of sexual orientation change, allowing me to fit into the world I wanted to belong to, seemed awfully good. But it still felt next to impossible most of the time.

That's where I was in my process of coming to terms with

my sexuality when I sat listening to Dennis Jernigan sing "Make Me More Free." Dennis was the first person I ever heard say that he struggled with same-sex attraction but was now married to a woman. And he had a bunch of kids. I'd never heard anything like that. I was overcome with both joy and terror. I felt joy hearing Dennis's experience. Yet I was also terrified at the thought of my friends, who had come to the concert with me, finding out why I was so excited by Dennis's story. I sat perfectly still, biting my cheek until it bled, trying not to blink so the tears wouldn't spill over and run down my face.

During that period I had perfected the art of hiding tears. They came so easily, but it was exhausting to try to contain them. It took every ounce of energy I had to keep from showing how moved I was by this testimony. If I had released the tension in my body for an instant, I would have crumpled into a sobbing mess as Dennis sang. It was the first time I felt even halfway understood. Dennis's story was *my* story.

When I heard "Make Me More Free" in that humongous Baptist church packed with people back in 1998, I was totally undone, because in my mind at that time, freedom meant the removal of these feelings that had burdened me for almost two decades of my life. The song gave me hope of freedom from my attraction to women, releasing me to be attracted to a man, and perhaps, in time, freedom to build a life that looked like Dennis's.

That was what the song meant to me then.

But on the Sunday morning I heard Pastor Pat singing it more than twenty years later in 2019, the song took on a very different meaning.

When Pat began singing "Make Me More Free," I instantly felt the tears well in my eyes, and I made no effort to stop them. Thankfully I no longer feel shame in crying, and that morning I let go. The tension in my body eased, and I felt a peace that could only be from God. All the anxiety I had felt praying on the drive to church that morning ceased. God had answered my prayer. God had given me my answer through that song. I knew it in the depths of my soul. He had made me "more free," yet again.

But what freedom in my life looks like is drastically different from what I had envisioned in 1998.

I asked God every day to take away anything, *anything*, that kept me from being who he wanted me to be. I believe he answered that prayer. The answer just didn't look like what I thought it would. For a long time, I sincerely believed, and stated often, that I wanted to stay open to however God desired to bless my life, including the possibility of entering into a relationship with a man. I sincerely tried to date godly men who knew about my attraction to women. While these men, whom I still consider friends, were very kind, any feelings I had for them waned in comparison to the feelings I experienced for women. And it wasn't long until I found myself drawn to a woman whom I came to love more deeply than I could have ever imagined.

So, on this Sunday morning in 2019, I found myself again asking God for direction, earnestly seeking to discern if being in a committed, monogamous relationship with this woman was a blessing from him or merely a temptation. Feelings of relief swept over me as I listened to Pat sing those familiar words. It was as though I actually heard God say to me, "It's okay, Sally, you're more free now. I want to free you from the burden it's been to believe that being in a relationship with someone of the same sex is immoral. You're free from living a life of aloneness. Being in a relationship with another woman, living in monogamous, faithful, covenant with her, is not out of reach for you. You're free to share your life with someone in that way."

If this had been the only moment in time that I had considered the possibility that same-sex relationships could be God honoring, I would understand anyone being skeptical of the sincerity of that moment. But it wasn't the first time. That moment was the culmination of more than two decades of my life spent searching for answers. Years of conversations with people whose opinions I trusted, and constant study and prayer, led me to this moment of believing two people of the same sex entering into a faithful, monogamous covenant relationship for life could be pleasing to God.

This reflects a shift from where I concluded my first memoir, *Loves God, Likes Girls*, published in 2013. In that book, which focuses primarily on my earlier life and relationship with my parents, I wrote, "I don't believe that being attracted to women was God's design for the expression of my sexuality. Nor do I believe that God intended for me to live out that expression in a sexual relationship with another woman." But I also said, "I find myself living in the tension, the unresolved conflict of what it is that God calls me to in this life, of what it means to take up my cross daily and follow him, and the longings to be in an intimate relationship with one person for life."[2] In other words, I was still wrestling with what I believed about same-sex relationships. I didn't think it was what God had in mind for me, but I also wasn't completely sure. As it turns out, God guided me in ways I didn't initially think possible. For the sake of younger generations who have been hurt by the church, for the sake of parents of LGBTQ children, for the sake of pastors and church leaders, I needed to write a sequel to tell the rest of the story.

Some of you will stop reading at this point, shaking your heads in disappointment, believing I simply gave in to accepting a different perspective in pursuit of my own desires. This is precisely why I wanted to write this book, to explain how I became affirming of same-sex relationships. It was an extensive process that took years, one that I never undertook with the intentional goal of becoming affirming. If anything, I set out determined to follow a traditional Christian sexual ethic. But in the end God showed me a different way. It wasn't merely a different interpretation of the key passages of Scripture regarding homosexuality. It wasn't a single book I read. It wasn't one conversation. It wasn't simply my own experience. Changing my mind about the morality of same-sex relationships was the culmination of all these things over a lifetime. How I came to be affirming, it turns out, started a long time ago, when the seeds of faith were first being planted in me.

Part 1

Practicing Hospitality

"'For I was hungry and you gave me something to eat,
I was thirsty and you gave me something to drink,
I was a stranger and you invited me in,
I needed clothes and you clothed me,
I was sick and you looked after me,
I was in prison and you came to visit me.'
Then the righteous will answer him,
'Lord, when did we see you hungry and feed you,
or thirsty and give you something to drink?
When did we see you a stranger and invite you in,
or needing clothes and clothe you?
When did we see you sick or in prison and go
to visit you?'
The King will reply,
'Truly I tell you, whatever you did for one of the least of
these brothers and sisters of mine, you did for me.'"

(Matt. 25:35–40, adapted)

1

Faith Roots

That Sunday morning when I heard "Make Me More Free" and understood it in a whole new way wasn't the first time I had considered that God could affirm a same-sex relationship. I had wrestled with the question for several years. Nor was it the first time my perspective changed on various practices that my faith community viewed as highly important. A significant change in thinking usually takes place over time. For example, it took me a while to see that Scripture does not prohibit dancing, having a glass of wine with dinner, or using instruments in worship. And it's okay for there to be more than two songs and a prayer before communion. Early in my understanding of what is and isn't permissible for a good Christian, I would have told you that all those things were wrong. But over time, I came to see them quite differently. This transformation didn't happen overnight, or even in a year. The spiritual journey of coming to believe the things we do takes a lifetime. In the same way, my belief that God might affirm a same-sex relationship only came after years of thoughtful reflection. In fact, that story begins before I was born.

My faith was first shaped by my parents and grandparents, the things they talked about and taught me, the places they took me, the experiences I had because I lived and spent my life with them. And they in turn were influenced by the faith of those that came before them. I don't come from generations of preachers and church leaders like some do, but I have a rich spiritual heritage, and my mom made sure I knew that. She spoke of her grandparents – my great-grandparents – on her mother's side going to church, and she told me about both of her parents teaching Sunday school. My grandmother was known for hosting luncheons for the ladies of their church, but more intriguing to me was her reputation for feeding migrant workers and drifters who wandered down from the train tracks in their small town. No sign hung on the back door of my grandmother's house, but they all knew where to go for something to eat. The tall, stout, brown-eyed woman was willing to share whatever she had during Depression times with anyone who came to the door.

One of my earliest memories is of my grandfather teasingly asking me whether I had learned my memory verse for "Pee Packers," a nickname he had coined for the kids group known as Pew Packers. Every Sunday night all the kids gathered at the front of the church and sat on the first pew while the preacher, Jimmy Jividen, went down the row with a microphone, giving each of us a chance to say the appointed verse of Scripture from memory. But PawPaw liked to joke and pretend he couldn't remember the name! While it might have seemed like mere play, the fact that PawPaw consistently asked me about Pew Packers indicated that he cared about me learning Scripture. And he was smart to engage a five-year-old with teasing.

My own parents also modeled a strong Christian faith and took me to church every chance they got. Every Sunday morning, every Sunday night, and every Wednesday evening we were there. Even if it was the one time of year that *The Sound of Music* was being aired on television at 6 p.m. on a Sunday night, we were still going to church. Because that's where we went to be spiritually fed and to fellowship and be encouraged and strengthened by fellow Christians. Before I ever started school, I knew this "church thing" was important. I knew it was the most meaningful part of our lives. It wasn't just about going to events or being part of a social gathering. It was about God – a God who loves and cares about us. From my earliest memories, God and our devotion to him were the center of everything.

Perhaps most formative for my faith were conversations with my mom. Maybe because she and I spent the most time together, especially in my early years. Mama told me stories all the time about her life and her growing-up years, and her faith was always intertwined with everything. She took her faith seriously at an early age and remained faithful to those convictions over her lifetime. To Mama, faith was the most important aspect of life, and her spiritual quest came to inspire my own. She often talked of walking to church on Sunday mornings with her family. They attended the First Baptist Church, first in Iowa Park and then in Holliday, two small Texas towns near the Oklahoma border. Both of her parents taught Sunday school. I've seen pictures of my grandfather posing with the young teenaged boys from his classes in the 1950s, with their hair slicked back with Brylcream and their jeans rolled up, like something out of a James Dean movie.

Mama loved to tell me about the time when her younger brother, about four or five years old, picked up a "horny toad" while walking to church and tucked it away in his pocket. Later, during the church service, he pulled it out and let it loose in the collection plate being passed around. My grandmother saw what he was doing. Realizing there were two elderly women at the other end of their pew who would be horrified at the sight of a horny toad in the collection plate, she quickly acted. But since the toad was running around in circles in the plate, it took some finesse on my grandmother's part to keep her composure while catching the chunky thing. In time she caught the toad and placed it in her purse, only to glance up and see the preacher glaring straight at her!

When Mama turned fourteen, she made the significant decision to begin attending a Church of Christ, where her boyfriend was a member. The Church of Christ grew out of the American Restoration Movement in the 1800s. It derives its name from Romans 16 where Paul says "all the churches of Christ send greetings" (v. 16). Led by Scotch-Irish-born Presbyterian minister's son Alexander Campbell (1788–1866), the Church of Christ has historically followed Campbell's desire to restore the New Testament church: that is, unity and conformity in the patterns of worship and in church governance in accordance with what is found in the New Testament. Campbell taught, "We speak only where the Bible speaks, and are silent where the Bible is silent." We weren't a man-made denomination, we were the "one true church," Christ's church. Despite Campbell's call to unity, his followers eventually branched into three separate bodies, the Church of Christ, First Christian, and Disciples of Christ.

My Baptist grandparents had no objections to my mom going to a Church of Christ with her boyfriend and his family, who were close friends of my grandparents. After a while Mama came home and announced that she wanted "to be baptized into the Church of Christ," and she hoped her parents would come to the baptism. My grandparents asked her questions, wanting to ensure that she was making the decision out of spiritual conviction, truly believing this was what God was calling her to do, and not on a whim because of a boy. Being satisfied with her answers and convinced that she wanted this for spiritually sound reasons, they accompanied her to the service. The church building didn't have a baptistry then, like most do today, so Mama was baptized in a river nearby. "I was baptized at night, and it's a good thing I didn't think of all the things that could've been in that creek bed I had to walk through, or I likely wouldn't have gone through with it!" my mom told me. She was petrified of snakes, so I knew she had to have been convinced that she needed to be immersed!

The week after my mother was baptized, my grandfather attended the monthly business meeting of the Baptist church where he and my grandmother were still members. At one point in the meeting a man started reading the names of people who were to be removed from membership for various reasons. When the group voted to remove his daughter, my grandfather got up and walked out, never going back. Years passed, Mama would say, before PawPaw went back to church. But every summer they would drive the car to different gospel meetings or tent revivals in the area, to listen to itinerant preachers. Marshall Keeble became one of my grandfather's favorites. It was Brother

Keeble, an African American preacher in the Church of Christ, who satisfied a white man's questions about grace and forgiveness sufficiently to draw PawPaw back to church. What started with a young girl visiting her boyfriend's church with his family led to a series of events that ultimately brought my entire family into the Church of Christ.

Mama continued to date the same boy she went to church with all through high school, and when they graduated, she decided to go with her boyfriend to Abilene Christian College (now Abilene Christian University), a small private school affiliated with the Church of Christ in West Texas. A girl going to college was a rarity in the 1930s. Men around town questioned my grandfather's judgment sending his daughter off to college, and a private one at that. "Why, Andy, you know she'll just go down there and get married! She won't work a day, and then you'll have wasted all that money paying for her education," my grandfather's friends would say. PawPaw was wiser than that. He knew the value of a college education for his daughter, whether she ever used the degree for a job outside the home or not. Mama did get married the summer after she graduated from college, but not to the boy she had dated in high school. And this is the part of the story that has always captivated me: what happened the very day she arrived on the campus of Abilene Christian in the fall of 1939. The boy she had followed down there broke up with her.

Lots of people, I'm sure, would have attributed her decision to go to a new church, and then her choice of colleges, to her relationship with the boy she had dated in high school. Therefore, when that relationship ended, people thought she'd return to the church of her youth, and that she'd certainly choose another college – one that was less expensive. Surely! But Mama stayed. She didn't leave Abilene Christian until her junior year, when her younger brother graduated from high school. Because their parents couldn't afford to send both of them to a private college, she and her brother enrolled at North Texas Teachers College, a less expensive public school now known as the University of North Texas. But she never left the Church of Christ.

My dad didn't grow up in a family of regular churchgoers. When I was growing up he would talk about occasionally attending local churches in the small West Texas communities where he lived. He visited the churches his relatives attended, too, and the family of one of his cousins went to a Church of Christ. Even as a boy he was paying attention to what was said from the pulpit. My dad told me about questioning the validity of what the preacher was saying – things like "only members of the Church of Christ are going to heaven." Daddy said he'd ask his cousin after the service whether or not he believed what the preacher had said, and his cousin told my dad that he didn't. My dad didn't either.

My dad's spiritual life had an impact on me, too, because I knew deep down inside – no matter what his behavior might have been like at times – he cared about being faithful. What that looked like might have been different for my dad, but it sent a message to me, loud and clear. Whether he was sitting at his desk in the study reading the Bible on Saturday nights, in preparation for the Sunday school class he was helping teach, or writing out a check to put in the collection plate the next morning, I knew these were his ways of being faithful to God. For most of my childhood, Daddy taught Bible classes, and he was always diligent about his preparation. He was equally diligent about pulling a dollar bill out of his wallet and handing it to me to put in the offering, after he dropped his check in, carefully folding it in half so that no one could see the amount.

Even though my dad was curious about faith in his younger years, his conversion – his actual coming to accept Jesus as Lord and Savior and his baptism – did not happen until after he met my mother. Mama would tell me about Daddy's tenderness toward the gospel, starting with his willingness to go to church with her on a Wednesday night for their first date. He even asked her to go with him to the nicest department store in town to buy a new pair of pants, because he didn't want to wear jeans or dungarees.

The weekend before they married, they were at the lake with some friends, waterskiing behind my dad's sporty green-and-white boat with the Johnson outboard motor. The boat that we still took to the lake every summer of my youth. My parents were both quite good at waterskiing and enjoyed going to the lake. It was a nice outing until the conversation turned more serious, eventually getting around to the fact that my father still hadn't been baptized, and it was only a week until the wedding.

If you were raised in the Church of Christ, especially during the late 1950s and early '60s, you had been taught that baptism by immersion was necessary for your salvation. If you hadn't been baptized, it didn't matter how staunchly you believed in Jesus being the Son of God, you still wouldn't be saved. And there are passages in Scripture about "not being yoked with unbelievers." Other verses in the New Testament talk about widows being allowed to marry, but only to believers. The Church of Christ interpreted these verses to mean that a "believer" was also someone who had been baptized. My mother took these passages very seriously.

"Aw, Betty, you don't have to be baptized to be saved," my dad said cockily while treading water alongside his boat in the middle of the lake.

Listening to this tale, I always cringed because I knew what was coming. Oh, Daddy, I would think, you shouldn't have said that! Then my dad would tell how my mom, who was sitting in the boat, took the oar that they brought just in case the motor went out, and started hitting the water all around my dad. He would laugh throughout the whole story, because he'd just said that to get a rise out of my mom, and he succeeded.

"I thought for a while she was gonna hit me in the head with that oar!" he'd say.

My mom would then tell the rest of the story, about how emotional my dad was when he was finally baptized. It was clear that my dad's decision to be baptized was his own, and not made solely because of my mother's insistence. I heard about the tears he shed coming up out of the water, and how people gathered around him to welcome him into the body of Christ.

Mama told me about a particular song that touched my dad when we sang it at church.

Years I spent in vanity and pride,
Caring not my Lord was crucified,
Knowing not it was for me he died
On Calvary!

Mercy there was great, and grace was free;
Pardon there was multiplied to me;
There my burdened soul found liberty
At Calvary.[1]

As a little girl, I watched the tears come easily to Daddy when we sang this song. I saw the tears he shed the Sunday night he "responded to the invitation" and "went forward" to ask for prayers to be a better husband and father. I was only five or six years old, but I have a vivid snapshot of Daddy's face, sobbing, surrounded by people comforting him. You see, my dad wrestled with anger, left over from a difficult childhood that left him feeling unloved and unwanted. That anger, pent up for so many years, often came out at my mom and me, and yet I still saw the goodness, the tenderheartedness in my dad. He served as a deacon and taught Sunday school classes all the time I was growing up, and he is faithful in his church attendance to this day.

Both of my parents modeled a strong faith, but Mama was the person I went to whenever I had a question about something that was in the Bible or was said at church. Talking about matters of faith or Scripture was so commonplace that I don't recollect specific conversations we had. I just know that from when I was a child riding home from church with my mom asking me about Sunday school to my college years when I came home for weekends, we talked nonstop about all that I was learning. Mama would always listen, and even when I brought up something she was hesitant about, she was still willing to hear more. As I grew older, I would ask her what the Bible said about a certain topic, and she would always tell me what she knew but quickly add, I'll study that and get back to you.

Mama had four different Bibles throughout my lifetime. The first Bible she had was absolutely falling apart before she replaced it. It took her forever to decide to get a new one, because the older one had so many notes and underlined passages and sermon outlines from years past. But with each new Bible came new notes, new passages to be underlined and starred with a pencil. For as long as I can remember, Mama carried a tiny red leather New Testament in the zipper compartment of her purse. It had passages marked, just like all her other Bibles. She had a larger Bible that she always took to church with her; she made notes in it and outlined the sermon. When we went on vacation, she packed her Bible in the suitcase, too. Very few pages in the Bible I have now that belonged to her are not marked in some way. The spine is broken, and many of the delicate, dog-eared pages are loose, indicating years of use.

Scripture was ingrained in me from the beginning as God's word to us about how to live, and even though it was written centuries ago, it had application for our lives today. I was rewarded for memorizing Scripture in my earliest years, and I was taught to use different passages as evidence, as "proof texts" to explain why we did something a certain way or refrained from doing something. Bible study was about finding the "right" answers, the "right" ways of doing things, with a sincere belief that our being right was also what was most pleasing to God. This tradition of interpretation of Scripture and having the right answers provided a sense of certainty that was comforting to me as a child.

My mom knew the right answers, but at the same time she was willing to admit when she didn't have an answer from Scripture, or when Scripture was puzzling. Mama was not one to force her opinion about the Bible on anyone. She was too gifted at persuasion for that. Mama was patient and an excellent listener. Like her parents, she allowed me to go to church with my friends, wherever they went. When I came home, I was always full of questions, processing what I'd heard and experienced in other places of worship and checking my discoveries against what I'd already been taught. Mama never got upset about any of it. She would simply draw me out and listen. I'm sure now that she learned at least some of that from her parents. Just as they supported Mama in her decision to become a member of the Church of Christ, so also Mama allowed me to seek and question and process, taking responsibility for my faith and what I believed.

2

Welcoming the Stranger

"Well, hello!" she would say as she scrunched into the backseat of our car. "Betty, Dan, how are you? And there's that Sally girl! How are you, little Sally?"

Before Carrye Smith ever opened the backseat door of the car, I could smell her perfume. Mama called it "old lady" perfume, because evidently it was a popular brand back in Carrye's younger days, when she would have first worn perfume. There was a whole section at church that smelled like that perfume. In fact, for a long time every church I ever walked into had women who smelled like that. Whenever we picked her up for church, I would hold my nose in anticipation as Carrye walked out of her house and started down the sidewalk. Mama would always make me put my hand down before Carrye got to where she could see what I was doing.

Every Sunday night for as long as I can remember, we picked up Carrye Smith on the way to church at six o'clock. Carrye was an elderly woman who had taught alongside my mom at Sam Houston Elementary School. She lived on a street that was right on our way to church, so it was easy to go by and pick her up. We had to leave a little earlier to accommodate the stop, but it was the least we could do, my mother always said.

Instead of laughing, Carrye cackled. Her voice was high pitched and shrill, and she laughed – or cackled – after nearly everything she said, whether it was funny or not. Since she had been an elementary teacher, she was always attentive to me. Carrye would ask me about school, and I always liked that she acknowledged my presence, even though I was a kid. But I wasn't *that* much of a kid, I said to myself. I was growing up. This old lady was still calling me "little Sally"! Oh, I did not like that. As I got older, the perfume, coupled with the insult of calling me "little" when she knew good and well that I was ten years old, made me dread going by to pick her up every week. But I was always nice. I knew who was sitting in the front seat.

Besides, this was something I'd grown accustomed to with my parents. My parents were always helping someone. Mama was always serving meals for bereaved families after a death, or preparing meals for people who were sick or elderly, long before we ever heard of Meals on Wheels. I always went with her, and she would talk to me in the car on the way about how we should act when we got to someone's home. If there had been a death, she would explain to me that the people inside were very sad, and it was important for me to be still and quiet when we got inside. If I knew the people, she would say, "They might like a hug."

An elderly man from our church lived around the block and down a street from us, and my mom loved going to visit him. Looking back on it now, I'm sure he reminded Mama of her dad, as he was about the same age as PawPaw would have been had he lived. I honestly don't know his first name – we just called him Brother Hardin. I was taught growing up to call all the adults at our church "Brother so-and-so" or "Sister so-and-so," because the church was our family. We would spend what seemed like hours at Brother Hardin's house when he would invite us over for lunch. Mama would ask him about how he cooked something, and we always went out to his backyard to compliment his flowers and his vegetable garden.

Brother Hardin might have been elderly, but he was still spry and active, his house was pristine, and he stayed busy doing things for others. He loved to cook, so every time we visited we had cake or cookies and iced tea or lemonade, if not a full-fledged lunch. When I had surgery in the seventh grade, after I came home from the hospital, Brother Hardin brought me lunch. He walked all the way from his house to ours, with a full tray of food, complete with dessert, silverware, and a cloth napkin; tiny salt and pepper shakers; and a slender vase with a rose from his garden. I felt very special.

The hospitality was mutual between Brother Hardin and us. And yet, as I grew older, I realized how much those visits must have meant to him. He was in his early eighties. His wife had passed several years earlier, and his children lived far away. His life was in caring for his home and in acts of kindness for someone else. I'm beginning to understand how much it must have meant to have my mom, who was about his daughter's age, bring her little girl round to visit and let him tell us about his garden and other stories from his past. At my young age, and with all the treats I received from him, I never dreamed we were giving, too. But we were.

My mother was a wonderful teacher in many ways, but perhaps one of her best "subjects" was empathy: the ability not only to feel *for* others but also to feel *with* them. Empathy isn't something that we're born with. It's not innate. Empathy must be learned. I learned from Mama, starting at a very young age, to think of how people might be feeling in different situations, or what their lives might be like, or what difficult circumstances they might have endured. But it didn't stop there. It wasn't enough to simply understand people's feelings. The greatest measure of empathy came in the form of hospitality, of welcoming the stranger, of making people feel valued and at home, especially people who didn't seem to fit anywhere. My parents were the best teachers I ever had in teaching me "radical hospitality," long before that phrase became a thing.

The very essence of Christianity is hospitality or the literal act of welcoming others. Dr. Richard Beck, professor at Abilene Christian University, writes, "It could be argued that hospitality – the welcoming of strangers – is the quintessential Christian practice. Welcoming sinners to table fellowship was a central, distinctive, and perhaps the most inflammatory aspect of Jesus' ministry and teaching."[1] This concept certainly wasn't foreign to me. I might not have heard the term "radical" as a descriptor of Christian hospitality until this century, but I'd been witnessing a unique version of it all my life. I'd observed my family in countless ways living out what hospitality to strangers looks like.

The hospitality that was modeled to me in my youth was clearly about welcoming strangers, people who didn't fit in with the rest of society for some reason, people who were disconnected and felt no sense of belonging. People who were invited into our home received acceptance, respect, and friendship. And in this space, "even if only briefly, the stranger is included in a life-giving and life-sustaining network of relations."[2] All my life I was encouraged to seek out the underdog, to befriend the new kid at school and make her feel welcome, to sit next to the visitor who didn't know anyone in my Sunday school class. I was taught to initiate conversation and friendship with the reticent and shy and to include those who had been excluded from the group. Both of my parents modeled this for me from a very young age.

A great part of my spiritual heritage and my theology of hospitality came from watching my mother and father welcome people. They lived out the gospel in front of me as they interacted with those who seemed to be forgotten. Our home was known for its warmth and a standing invitation to drop by. The television would be turned off, and guests would be offered something to eat and drink. It might simply be leftovers out of the refrigerator, but Mama would always find something to serve. She had learned that from her mom and dad, who were also known for opening up their home to family and friends, to the Sunday school classes they taught, and to the drifters that came by for a meal.

During the 1930s, my grandparents lived in a shotgun house down by the railroad tracks in the small north Texas town of Holliday. They were invested in their community. My grandfather served on the school board and worked for Sinclair Oil. His job required him to walk a long stretch of pipeline that ran between Holliday and Electra, Texas. The landscape in that part of north Texas is dry and desolate, covered in cactus and mesquite trees. It's scorching hot in the summer, and the cold, dry wind that blows in the winter will freeze your lips together. Armed with a loaded revolver for the very real threat of rattlesnakes or coyotes, my grandfather set out early every morning and didn't return until dinner time. Meanwhile, in town, my grandmother had her own beauty salon, where women would pay a dime to have their hair "set" and a whole quarter for a permanent wave. In those days of the Great Depression, it was regarded as miraculous that my grandfather had consistent work, let alone a wife who owned her own business.

"We always had meat on the table for dinner," Mama told me. "It might've been a rabbit Daddy shot on the way home from work, but at a time when a lot of people didn't have food, we always had something to eat."

In the midst of the Great Depression, my grandparents were hospitable, sharing what they had with neighbors. They were poor themselves, even though both worked. Having little to share, though, didn't keep them from giving to others who were less fortunate and obviously in need. "Loving your neighbor" included the drifters and migrant workers, as my grandmother would later recall, who would jump off a passing railroad car and wander over to their back door looking for anything to eat. Word spread quickly that the people who lived in my grandparents' house would feed you. Whether it was leftovers or whatever happened to be cooking at the time, there was always enough to share with whoever showed up at the back door. Regardless of race or how the person was dressed or how recently the person had bathed, Granny would feed anyone who asked.

Mama remembered, at times, finding a small crowd of five to ten shabbily dressed, unshaven men sitting out on the stoop of their house, just outside the kitchen, eating a plate of food her mother had prepared.

"My own grandparents," Mama often told me, "owned a boarding house, and my mother grew up learning to cook for large groups of people, serving them at the long dining table. Nobody could cook better than Big Grandma." My great-grandparents were so known for caring for people in their community that when a doctor in town delivered a baby to a young underage girl who wasn't able to care for the child, he brought the newborn to their house. Taking one look at the baby boy, Big Grandma cradled him in her arms and took him inside. My granny, then only four years old, now had a younger brother to play with, named Leonard.

This gift of generosity was passed down from long ago, becoming a natural part of the overarching gift of hospitality displayed in my great-grandparents, my grandparents, and my parents. It's as though welcoming and caring for people on the margins became grafted into our DNA. And by the time it was my turn, showing hospitality was as natural as breathing.

The home I grew up in was at times a revolving door for people who didn't seem to fit anywhere else. Our house was full of women attending bridal and baby showers on Sunday afternoons, balancing plates of iced thumbprint cookies, white cake, and pastel butter mints with cups of lime sherbet and ginger ale punch on their laps, oohing and aahing as the bride or mom-to-be opened each gift. We hosted parties for friends' children graduating high school and going off to college. We would sweep our patio clean, borrow tables and chairs from the church and set them with tablecloths and centerpieces, and string up paper streamers made out of the school's colors catty-corner across the top of the patio. Freshly graduated from high school, incoming college freshmen invited their friends to join in the festivities.

At least once a year, my dad's Sunday school class for men and women enlisted in the air force met at our house for a party. When Daddy began teaching a budget course for officers and taught students from all over the world, we always had his classes over to our house for dinner. Mama would find out where the students were from and try to prepare foods from their home countries. We'd set up the Ping-Pong table on the patio and horseshoes in the backyard, and they would play for hours. No one ever left our house hungry.

Some of the single individuals at church naturally gravitated toward us because my parents purposely sought them out. As a result, they would often stop by on a weekday evening, just to visit. Sometimes they would literally raid the refrigerator and eat whatever we had left over for dinner. Some would come specifically to talk to my mom, who might as well have been a licensed counselor, as much as she listened to people. She would take them into the living room where it was quiet and away from my dad and me, who were back in the den watching television.

Growing up, I watched my parents wrestle with drawing healthy boundaries for our family and those they ministered to. There were times when we needed to care for ourselves, to rest and be rejuvenated, and so my parents would have to say no to caring for others on occasion. But much of the time, my parents were there to volunteer at church for whatever needed to be done, whether it was taking food to someone who was sick or housing students who were traveling through town or driving students to visit Christian college campuses. We were the family you could count on to help with anything.

My parents seemed to have especially tender hearts for people who were alone – single individuals, people who were divorced, abandoned children. Some of my earliest and, as it turns out, most formative memories revolved around caring for people in these circumstances. Like the Shuberts, whose husband and father left a family of four children and a mom who had never held a job outside her home. Moms without jobs outside the home were common in the 1960s. Families without fathers were not, especially families in churches. But this woman came with her four kids every Sunday, bringing them to Bible classes, and sitting in the same section of the auditorium for services as we did. I don't know how long my parents had known Ethel Shubert, but they were always friendly to her at church. Mama would stand and talk with her after services were over, and my dad, who has always made a point to talk to teenagers, would tease and cut up with the oldest two children who were in his Sunday school class.

One evening before I ever started to school, the Shuberts came over for dinner at our house. The oldest son, Paul, had just graduated from high school and had been drafted into the army to fight in Vietnam. He was to ship out in a few days, so Mama invited the whole family for a farewell dinner for Paul. Because I was so young at the time, I only have snapshot memories of the meal, but I remember distinctly eating off of card tables in the den. I don't know why my mom didn't set the table for all of us in the dining room. Maybe there wasn't enough room to seat all eight of us. But I remember distinctly the coziness of that meal. The laughter and conversation between and among two tables of four. The embrace of a divorced woman and her four children. For a long time after, my mom and dad would talk about how ravenously the children ate, as though they hadn't had a meal in days. We wondered at every meal how they were doing.

The following Christmas, Paul was in Vietnam, and their family had very little income. My father had just changed jobs to have better hours for family life. He began teaching at Sheppard Air Force Base in civil service, resulting in less salary. But despite not having very much, what my parents did that Christmas for the Shuberts made an impression on me. One evening the week of Christmas, my mom and dad loaded up the car and we went over to the Shuberts' house. It took a while to load the car because we were taking a real Christmas tree that we bought at the Optimist Club lot downtown, along with everything needed to decorate the tree. We also took a present for each member of the family, hot chocolate, and other goodies to snack on while we played Christmas music and decorated their tree. People were laughing, chomping, singing, and reaching for ornaments, while my mom untangled the lights for the tree. It's one of my favorite memories of childhood. Again, because I was so young, it's just a snapshot memory, but it's one that deeply embedded itself in my soul at a crucial time in my development, at an age when I was beginning to discern who my family was, what we were about, who I was to be.

Not long after that, when I was about five years old, I accompanied my mom to the home of a family whose mother had passed away. Mostly I remember the sparse back bedroom where the children were playing. Seated on bare mattresses made of cotton ticking, two of the children whose mother had died were playing a game with their hands. Facing each other, one of them held his hands palms down out in front of him, while the other held her hands palms up, underneath her brother's hands. Then she would try to reach up quickly and slap the back of her brother's hands before he could move them. The other kids in the room were all standing around watching, rooting for one or the other to win. That's one of the snapshots I see in my recollection of that day. Next, we're shopping at Treasure City, a local discount store like Walmart or Target, my mom and I and all three of the children who had lost their mom. But a lot happened in between those snapshots of a five-year-old's memory.

It would be much later in my life before I came to fully appreciate what my parents did that day for the Price family and the profound impact it had on me. I've come to believe that day and the year that followed were pivotal in how I look at the totality of the gospel. That day I witnessed my parents live out what Jesus said were the two greatest commands, to love God with all your heart, soul, mind, and strength, and to love your neighbor as yourself. For my parents, love for God and neighbor meant taking in the Price children for almost a year.

We first came to know the Price family, a mom and her three children, because they went to our church. Mrs. Price was divorced from her husband, who was also the father of her children. They were an extremely poor family who lived in government housing and lived off the wages Mrs. Price earned looking after neighbor kids in her home day care. Being only five, I don't know that I ever knew why Mrs. Price died. I just remember thinking how awful it would be to not have a mother anymore. We had been acquainted with the family for a couple of years before her death, and the children were familiar with us. In fact, about a year before his mother's death, the middle son asked if I would enter the "big brother/little sister" contest with him at the Boys Club. My mom agreed and dressed me up in a red dress and red patent leather shoes. Our families sat together to watch Tommy and me walk across the stage when they called our names. We didn't win, but that was okay.

When Mrs. Price died, Tommy was in my dad's Wednesday night class for boys at church, so my parents learned of it right away. My mom agreed to help, alongside other women at church, to serve dinner for the Price family on the day of the funeral. I don't remember what she brought, but she came home with more than her pots and pans. The oldest Price child, a girl just fourteen years old, and her two brothers, ages thirteen and eleven, gathered their belongings and got in our car with us.

When I was older, I learned about the conversation my mom overheard between the Price children's father and grandmother. While helping to clean up the kitchen after everyone had finished eating, my mom heard them discussing who was going to take the children.

"My wife just isn't up to taking care of kids," the dad, who had divorced Mrs. Price, said of his new wife. "So I can't take them."

The grandmother responded, "Well, I can't take them either.

At my age, with all the drugs and trouble teenagers can get into. I can't take care of them. I'm too old for all that."

I can only imagine how the rest of the conversation went as my mother interjected her own thoughts. All I know is that those kids I had been playing with left with Mama and me. But before we went home together, my mom went into the drab, brick-walled bedroom where the boys normally slept. They had a few items of clothing that we loaded into brown paper grocery sacks, since they had no suitcase. Mama looked around in the bathroom for toiletries and riffled through the old chest of drawers for underwear and socks. What she found was so old that she told them to just come on, we'd get whatever they needed at the store. And the next thing I remember is riding in the cart at Treasure City with Mama piling packages of underwear, toothbrushes, toothpaste, and deodorant into the back of the cart behind me.

At some point she called my dad to tell him what she had done – that she had brought three basically orphaned children home with her. Children for whom she had no legal guardianship. But I don't think anything would have kept Mama from taking the Price kids with us that afternoon. And as she would later proclaim, "I didn't know what Dan would say, but I just couldn't leave those kids." My dad acted like it was the most natural thing in the world for these three kids we knew from church to be sitting in the den when he arrived. That's the way I remember him acting for the whole time they were there. He played with the boys, Tommy and Tony; helped the older girl, Deanne, practice driving to get her license (allowed at that age for hardship reasons); and ate dinner with us every night.

Most nights I slept with Deanne in the big double bed in my room. Since our house had just two bedrooms and only one bathroom, the boys slept on the sleeper sofa in the den. Every night my mom helped them make out the bed, and every morning when we got home from taking everyone to school, she stripped the soaked sheets off and put them in the washer, later hanging them out to dry. The youngest boy wet the bed, Mama said, every night they were in our home. But it was never mentioned. In fact, I'm not sure my dad ever knew. Mama would always say, "It's no wonder, given what he's been through."

Mrs. Price had made the eldership of our church the executor of her will, and eventually it was decided that the children would live at Tipton Children's Home in Oklahoma. This was a hard decision, made in part because of my parents' economic situation. We had all grown to love each other as family. The two oldest children, especially, played with me and were incredibly good to me. I loved them like a brother and a sister. As we drove back after leaving the three children at Tipton, we rode with all the windows down, the wind blowing our hair and drying the tears that ran down my mother's cheeks. Our only solace was that the Price kids would spend the holidays and summers with us for the next several years.

It wasn't until I was much older that I realized, and even now more so, how much that experience influenced me. Namely, that one of my earliest memories is of my parents modeling the unconditional love of God for all those kids.

They lived out the biblical call of "caring for the orphans and widows."

They allowed God to "place the lonely" in their family.

They demonstrated sharing whatever they had, when it meant they had less.

They welcomed Jesus in the form of three children who weren't theirs.

And in doing so, they showed me how to live out the radical love and hospitality that Jesus displayed while he lived here on this earth. Having this example in my bank of experience for a lifetime has enabled me to see those stories of Jesus welcoming strangers, children, misfits, women, lepers, tax collectors – everyone the religious leaders deemed unwelcome – as a normal way of life.

Yet in my humanness, in the busyness of my world, I can easily forget. Then in times of plenty, I focus my attention on gaining more for myself. And in times of uncertainty and want, I can begin to believe that I must hold on to what I have, lest I need it for myself. Even when the concept of radical hospitality is so deeply ingrained in me, I can forget that Jesus calls me to a hospitality far beyond the secular legal standard of what an "ordinary, reasonable, prudent person" would do.[3] I can forget that radical hospitality is the parable of the good Samaritan, who gives without one moment of hesitation to the person who is in need, going the second mile to care for needs beyond today without looking for accolades or repayment. I can forget that radical hospitality is the early church in Acts who "sold property and possessions to give to anyone who had need" (Acts 2:45). And I can even forget that radical hospitality is God come to earth to experience life among us and save us from ourselves.

Welcoming the stranger is what I'm called to as a follower of Christ. My parents taught me that.

What I didn't know while growing up is how much I would need that welcome for myself, and how it would shape God's call on my life to offer hospitality to people my church community often deemed untouchable.

3

Looking in the Mirror and Seeing the Stranger

For the longest time I knew I was different from other kids, but at first, I didn't realize my difference had to do with sexuality. In the Bible Belt of the 1960s and '70s, people just didn't talk about anything having to do with sex, and they certainly didn't mention anything about same-sex relationships. All I knew was, I was drawn to certain girls in a different way than I was to boys.

It wasn't that I didn't care for boys. I liked them too. But as I came to realize later, it was not the same kind of "like" that I felt for girls. When I was in junior high, a boy named Kenneth caught my eye. He played the trombone in the band, and I was in the clarinet section. He had the most beautiful dark, curly hair and brown eyes, and I loved the days he paid attention to me. We made silly faces at each other during rehearsal, and I prayed that our paths would cross when the bell rang and we were putting our instruments up. Then we would oh-so-subtly end up walking to our next class together. We remained good friends for years and dated off and on through high school, attending prom together. I had wonderful times with Kenneth. But I never had the intense romantic feelings for him or any boy that I went out with in high school or college that I felt for a girl.

Being a teenager and having no resources to help me understand the difference in my sexual orientation, I didn't know how to articulate what set me apart from my female friends. I just thought, "What's all the boy fuss about?" The pervasive girl talk about "liking" boys, dating, kissing, and falling in love felt wasted on me at the time. Not that I didn't experience an interest in and curiosity about sex, because I did. But I kept that to myself.

My sex education consisted of gossip at sleepovers; two brief conversations with my mom in the fifth and eighth grade, respectively; popular movies; and crude innuendos from boys on the junior varsity football team. At one sleepover, my friends and I sat mesmerized as we read from *Ode to Billy Joe*, the cheap and tawdry paperback novel that was based on the song. Then there was the fifteen-year-old girl in biology class who relished telling me about her sexual exploits.

I remember hearing that when a girl likes a boy "like that," she typically got all fidgety and nervous around him. Her mouth might get dry, and she might feel tongue-tied and awkward in his presence. Her heart rate would increase and her palms sweat, or she might feel all these things at once, simply from thinking about him. "Huh," I pondered to myself. "I wonder what that's like?" Even more, I would think, "Maybe there's something wrong with me because I've never felt that way around Kenneth."

In fact, I didn't feel that awkward nervousness around anyone until my sophomore year in high school, in my geometry class.

I don't remember the exact moment I noticed her. There was no clash of cymbals as the orchestra broke into a rendition of "Ah, sweet mystery of love, at last I've found you!" No birds tweeting, announcing the opening of spring, and thus beckoning first loves. I just remember becoming more and more aware of this girl who sat one seat in front of me on the row right next to mine.

Shelli had short, dark hair in the Dorothy Hamill style popular in the mid-1970s. Petite and always dressed as cute as a button, Shelli was quiet and reserved and only spoke if I said something to her first. Of course, I became tongue-tied around her, so most of the time I didn't speak to her at all. One of my guy friends from band sat directly in front of me, though, so I could talk comfortably to him and sometimes get her attention that way. Day after day I tried to impress Shelli with my wit, and if I could get the least little smile out of her, it was a good day.

I had no idea at the time why I felt the way I did when I was around her. I didn't fully grasp that what I was feeling indicated a "crush," but looking back, it most definitely was. At the time, I didn't associate my feelings with anything romantic, and I didn't feel any kind of sexual attraction to Shelli. I just knew what I felt was entirely different from anything I had ever felt around anyone.

Once when I was riding in the passenger seat with my mom at the wheel, we pulled up beside Shelli's car at a stoplight. My heart started racing, hoping and willing her to look over at me. Simultaneously, I was terrified she actually would look over and see me riding with my mother in a 1970 yellow station wagon with wood-grain paneling (yes, exactly like the car Chevy Chase trades in for demolition in the movie *Vacation*). Of course, her car was also vintage, just cooler to me at the time – a huge, brown, two-door Lincoln Continental with a cream ragtop, a regular land barge. The windows of Shelli's car were rolled down and the radio station every teenager in Wichita Falls listened to, KTRN, was blasting the latest hit from ABBA. "You are the dancing queen, young and free, only seventeen!" From then on, "Dancing Queen" became our song. To this day, I can't hear it without thinking of the girl from geometry class.

The next time a girl made my heart flutter was during my senior year in high school. Yet I still didn't connect the feelings I had for her to my sexuality. I didn't know anything about sexual orientation. But I knew even then that I was drawn to this girl in a way I never was to a boy. My heart pounded when she walked into our Sunday school classroom. I wanted to sit next to her, but I was always nervous and self-conscious. If I sat next to her at church, I would practically melt because she had the most beautiful voice. Besides that, she was drop-dead gorgeous. She didn't seem to have a lot of friends, though, so I tried to befriend her. I was a year ahead of her in school, so I thought it would be good to start inviting her to do things with the rest of the youth group after church on Sunday nights.

One night we were walking across the parking lot from the youth building at our church to the main auditorium when I noticed something shiny on the asphalt. I stopped to take a closer look and realized it was a gold ring with an oval black onyx stone. When I reached down to pick it up, she snatched it out of my hand and tried it on one of her fingers.

"It looks like a guy's class ring, doesn't it?" she said, holding her hand out in front of her, looking at the oversized ring on her forefinger.

"Well, it's a little big, all right," I commented, but already I was scheming up plans for that ring.

I took it home and found some glitter glue. On the black onyx stone, I drew a capital letter *R*, in gold glitter, for our high school, Rider. Then I found some red yarn to twirl around the back of the ring, so that it would fit a smaller finger than originally intended. When I finished, it was a pretty good replica of a boy's senior ring from S. H. Rider High School. The next time I saw Molly, I brought the ring and pretended to give it to her as a "go steady" gift. Other friends were around watching as I pulled off the prank, with Molly playing right along.

Most of the time we simply interacted as friends, but Molly wore the ring I gave her, so sometimes we played the parts, breaking into a fight over something that two people in a romantic relationship would get upset over. Yet this was always in front of people to get a laugh. There was never a time that a romantic vibe existed between Molly and me, and certainly nothing physical. As far as Molly was concerned, we were nothing more than friends. What I didn't tell her or anyone else was how I felt about those staged exchanges between us. I didn't understand why that pretend relationship felt more natural and exciting to me than any dating experience I had had with a boy. I assumed that would change as I got older. Maybe someday if I met the right boy, I would feel that way about him. But it never happened.

The first time I ever felt sexually aroused by the thought of a woman was the fall of my sophomore year in college. I had a dream about kissing a girl. It scared me, and at the same time it was exhilarating. I had no earthly idea what that meant because in 1981 in Abilene, Texas, nobody had any idea about sexual orientation, or if they did, they certainly weren't talking about it. I just figured that everybody must experience some degree of sexual attraction to their own gender and concluded that's all this dream meant. I kept trying to tell myself it was nothing more than some kind of phase I was going through. But the memory of that kiss remained.

In the dream I was on a date with a woman, sitting in the front seat of a car with her at a drive-in movie. I don't remember what was playing on the screen, but I remember her vividly. I knew exactly who she was in the dream, a tall, slender, beautiful auburn-haired woman who was eager to kiss me. I knew her, but I couldn't recall her name, nor could I remember how I had come to know her. That scared me even more, thinking that she might be someone on campus and I wouldn't remember until I ran smack-dab into her! How awkward would that be? As if I could tell her, "Hey, funny thing the other night, I dreamed we kissed!" That would not have been the least bit humorous in 1981. Not at all.

At Abilene Christian, on certain nights of the week, popular television shows drew huge crowds of students in the dorm lounge. *Mork & Mindy* was a brand-new show that starred Robin Williams. We all loved it. Robin Williams, with his unparalleled wit and improvisational skills, was a treat, especially to eighteen- and nineteen-year-olds. Plus, it was a cheap date. One day as we all sat there watching, I suddenly remembered who the girl was. Robin Williams's costar, Pam Dawber! As my face grew flush, I prayed no one could see just how embarrassed I was at the thought of kissing Mindy. At the same time, I was relieved that it wasn't anyone I knew in real life. Yet, I was taken aback by how moved I was by the kiss itself.

Why couldn't I get it off my mind? Was it because I had kissed a woman, even if in a dream, and it felt good and completely natural – more so than with any boy I had ever kissed? (Not that there was a whole busload lined up down the hall.) Or was I consumed by those thoughts because I felt guilty for merely thinking about kissing another woman, let alone actually doing it? I never asked those questions to anyone. It was too risky. What would they think of me for having such a dream? But a dream it was. A dream completely out of my control.

I never shared what was going on inside me with anyone. Not even my mom, even though I had a very sweet, trusting relationship with Mama, for as long as I could remember. She was my confidante in every other respect. But I could never bring myself to talk to her about these oddities I had noticed about myself since adolescence. I couldn't dare risk telling her something that would undoubtedly alter the nature of our relationship forever, if not completely destroy it. Or so I believed at the time. I began thinking that these feelings could mean something about me that I didn't yet want to name or face. I couldn't bear the thought of disappointing Mama, so I never shared any of this with her – or anyone – until much later.

In my junior year of college, I began putting the pieces together. I thought what I was experiencing might mean that I was homosexual, the only word I knew at the time to describe what I was feeling for another woman. But I wasn't certain of that. I hoped with all my heart that it didn't mean that. In 1982, though, there was very little open conversation about sexuality on a Christian university campus, and even less about sexual attraction between two people of the same sex. I had no idea what to think. I had no resources save for the books I took off the shelves of the library that were a decade or two old.

As I recalled the derogatory names I heard directed at certain people who experienced the same attractions as me, I felt absolutely humiliated taking those books off the shelf. But I had to find out what was happening to me. Reading books and journal articles in the library was the only way I could learn about something so foreign, at least without having to reveal this deeply strange and unfolding secret about me to an adult. I had never heard anyone specifically talk about same-sex relationships from a Christian perspective, except for my freshman Bible professor simply answering a student's question as to "when homosexuality becomes a sin." Beyond that, I had no one I felt I could go to who would be both compassionate and knowledgeable about my predicament.

The stories I had heard about fellow students being found out and expelled from school were fresh and raw, and I couldn't risk that. So, I gathered the materials I could find in the library and began slinking my way, hopefully unnoticed, to a table hidden in the far back recesses of the library. Reading the words "homosexual" and "homosexuality" over and over, with a growing awareness that what I was reading was meant to refer to me, filled me with shame. I was beginning to see that the feelings I had been experiencing were indicative of my being attracted to the same sex. I couldn't stand the thought of being called a homosexual, a clinical term for people whose sexuality had become so distorted, so perverted, that, not long ago, shock therapy and chemical castrations had been performed on them. This is what I took away from my study, at a secluded table in the library, on a university campus, praying no one would find me.

Not mentioned in any of the reading I did that day was something I already knew. I knew that my feelings were not of my own volition. I did not choose to be attracted to girls. I didn't even know how to choose that, didn't know there was an option to choose. I was fifteen years old when I noticed a girl in a different way for the first time. To say that my attraction was a choice at any age, but especially at the young age of fifteen, is cruel. Such a belief reflects the lack of understanding we had about sexuality when I was growing up. And sadly, it's still a prevalent myth in many Christian circles.

From the moment I realized during my junior year of college that what I was experiencing indicated a true sexual attraction to someone of the same sex, I prayed to God to take those feelings away. I prayed that same prayer for the next fifteen years. But God never did remove those attractions. During that time, I held to what I had been taught to believe all my life, that acting on sexual desire with someone of the same sex is immoral. But the desire to share my life with a woman, to love and be loved by another woman, never faded.

For the next fifteen years I didn't tell a soul that I was attracted to women. I tried everything I knew to distract myself from the growing loneliness and misery I often felt being alone. I threw myself into coaching competitive speech and debate for ten years. I enjoyed teaching and loved being with students, believing in the importance of the skills they were developing in my classroom. But at the same time, I was restless. With each passing year after graduate school, I became more and more disillusioned with the idea of meeting a man that I would actually want to marry.

By the time I fell seriously in love again with a woman, I had stopped teaching and had entered law school at Texas Tech. Although my friend never knew the depths of my feelings for her at the time, she was well aware of my erratic behavior toward her. I was unable to explain my reasons for being jealous of her dating relationship with the man she planned to marry. When she asked me to be in the wedding, I tried to be a good friend to her at that important time in life, including hosting a shower for her. But all of that took its toll on me and left me in a deeply depressed state.

One night I was so miserable that instead of studying for a law exam, an exam that would determine my grade for the semester, I sat down and wrote a long letter to God. I felt shame as I used the word I hated most to describe myself, "homosexual," wanting to be totally open and honest with God, maybe for the first time. Night turned into morning, and I missed the big exam, but finally, I was laying all of me before God, without my own agenda for taking care of this. Desiring God's leading, I prayed, "What do you want me to do?"

I decided to seek help and made a phone call to a Christian counselor in Dallas. I was able to schedule an appointment for the next week. Driving there was the scariest thing I had done up to that point in my life. I knew that once I got there, I would have to tell him why I was there. I was there because I was attracted to women and I didn't want to be. I hadn't chosen this, and I had no idea where it came from or how I got here. I'll never forget the moment I was received by this man I barely knew at the time. David didn't change the loving expression on his face. He didn't refer me to someone else because "this" wasn't his expertise. He didn't get out his Bible and read the passages from Genesis, Leviticus, Romans, 1 Corinthians, or 1 Timothy to me. He welcomed me, with the unconditional love of Jesus.

For the last year and a half of law school, I flew once a week from Lubbock to Dallas to talk with the counselor. David's hospitality in those first several months made the grueling sessions more bearable. In those first sessions, I agonized primarily about when and how I would tell my parents. I was scared to death of how they would respond. Would my mom and dad respond like a dear friend's family had responded to him when he came out? My friend's family stopped all communication, all contact with him, after they discovered he was gay. I was horrified at what he must be going through being cut off from all his family like that. Not just his parents, but his siblings and grandparents and aunts and uncles and cousins.

My grandparents were no longer living, but I had extended family I was very close to, so this hit me hard. Being an only child, my cousins were like siblings to me. I could not fathom being separated from them like that. It literally made me sick to my stomach. Stories of gay friends in Christian families like mine had reinforced my decision to keep my sexuality a secret all these years. And now, as I was contemplating how to share this news with my own family, these experiences of my friends certainly didn't provide any comfort or reassurance. I was scared to death.

But I knew I needed to tell my parents. I wanted to tell them now, after all the years of going through this alone. I had reached a point of such misery that I was willing to do whatever it took to feel better. And it seemed this was the next right thing to do.

After several months of meetings, David and I decided it would be best for me to talk to my mom alone. All my life I had been closer to my mother than to my father, so I felt more comfortable talking to her first. Mother's Day was coming up, so I invited Mama to visit me for the weekend in Lubbock. I explained that it would be more difficult for me to come home, given that I was in the middle of law school exams. She agreed, and spunky seventy-five-year-old that she was, she drove out to Lubbock all by herself.

Fearful of her rejection or, at the very least, a drastic change in the way she related to me, I prolonged the agony of telling Mama until Sunday night, before she was planning to go home Monday morning. That way, I thought, if she didn't take my revelation well, we wouldn't have to experience the awkwardness for long. As always, we got up that Sunday morning and went to church where I had placed membership during my first year of law school, the Broadway Church of Christ. I liked it there.

The building and the people who attended reminded me of the church I grew up in, the Tenth and Broad Church of Christ in Wichita Falls, Texas. Every Sunday I was met with hugs from Rob Corey, one of the elders, and friendly greetings from the couples in the small group I joined. Rod Blackwood and Larry

Christian, two of the elders at Broadway, had come to see me at my apartment one evening after I had first visited the church. That meant the world to me as a single person. I placed membership at Broadway the following Sunday and always felt at home there.

That Sunday morning was like so many Sunday mornings in my life, sitting next to Mama at church. Hearing her strong alto voice took me back to an earlier time, when she used to hold the hymnal and point to the words, teaching me to sing. This woman had taught me everything I first learned about church, from being quiet and not disturbing others who were trying to listen to the sermon, to being friendly and greeting visitors. This was the woman who had rocked me to sleep from infancy, singing "We Shall See the King Someday." Her deepest desire for me was to know Jesus and to follow God's will for my life. Her approval mattered more to me than anyone's, and on that Sunday morning I feared her disapproval more than I ever had in my life. I was a bundle of nerves.

After church, we went to eat lunch, and fortunately the wait for a table was long, helping to drag out the time until I was going to have to tell her. I felt like my life as I knew it was about to come to an end. And yet, there was a part of me deep down inside that couldn't imagine Mama turning her back on me, to any degree. Especially if she understood that I didn't choose this, that I had no idea how this happened, that it was beyond my control. Most of all, I believed she would understand when I assured her that I still wanted whatever God desired for my life.

I think I felt this reassurance because so many of the people I had watched Mama love throughout my lifetime were cast out by certain segments of society. She loved on people who were poor, sharing not only her wealth but also her friendship. She loved people who were divorced at a time when it was unheard of to be divorced in the church. She loved people who had all kinds of problems, who were socially awkward and seemed to have no place to fit. I watched her take in kids with no home and spend hours listening to people who sought her counsel. And now, about to reveal my secret, I was thinking specifically of how she had responded to her brother's son, when it was revealed in hushed conversation that he was gay.

Mama never changed the way she treated him, nor the ways in which she spoke of him. Her love remained, as it did for friends of mine who eventually came out. Whenever I'd tell her that a friend had come out, Mama always said, "Well, we love _____ (fill in the friend's name). We just keep loving them." And when I told her about my friend's family who had abandoned him, I remember Mama shaking her head, saying, "Oh my goodness. I just don't know how anybody could do that. That's your baby. I don't care what they've done!" I remember her words so exactly, and the expression on her face, because I was listening for me. I was listening to how she would respond to me.

Still, I worried on this Mother's Day Sunday. It's different when it's *your* daughter. Even with all those examples of my mom's hospitality to others over my lifetime, I still couldn't be sure that her response to me would be the same. First, we were talking about something that I knew she considered to be against God's will, and second, we were talking about *her child*, a child she believed she would answer to God for her raising. Because of those two factors, I had no guarantee of a positive outcome.

That night as we finished eating supper and began clearing the table, I looked for a way to start the conversation. This was a routine I had experienced with my mom so many times in my life – bringing all the dishes from the dinner table back into the kitchen and stacking them in the sink to be rinsed before putting them in the dishwasher. Mama started rummaging around for a plastic container to put leftovers in while I started filling the dishwasher. It didn't take long for the two of us, working together, to finish. We wiped off the countertops and headed into the living room. I began telling Mama about the counseling I was receiving from David in Dallas. When I first started going, I told her that I was seeing a counselor to work through relationship struggles with my dad. That was true, but now I wanted to share more of why I was going.

"Mama, you know I've been talking to David about Daddy, right?"

She sat down on the edge of an ottoman she had given me when I moved into my first apartment.

"Yeah," she said, looking up at me.

"Well, I've needed to talk to him about more than that, and I don't know how to tell you about it," I continued, sitting down on the other end of the ottoman, back to back with Mama so she couldn't look at me. I didn't want to see her face when I told her, fearful of seeing disappointment and despair in the eyes of the most important person to me.

"It's okay, you can tell me anything," she replied, but I heard the hesitance, the worry in her voice already.

"Do you remember that time I was so upset in graduate school, feeling like I had lost a friend, and you and Daddy came down to spend a weekend with me to talk about why I was so upset?" I asked her, feeling the shame rising up in my chest. But before she could answer, I nervously blurted it out.

"Mama, I had feelings for her. Feelings that went much further than just friendship. I don't understand why I did, but I did, and I was heartbroken when it felt like she pulled away from me. And now, years later, I have feelings for another friend that are more like romantic feelings, and it scares me to death to tell you that because I don't want to be that way. I just am." My words rushed out and tears began to form. "I don't know what to do about it! I don't want you to not love me! I couldn't stand that!"

It only took a second for Mama to respond, but my stomach clenched, wondering what she would say.

Gently, Mama got up off of her end of the ottoman and came around to face me. "Well, honey, my goodness. Mama would never not love you." As she reached down to hug me, she looked at me and said, "You couldn't tell me anything that would make me stop loving you."

I burst into sobs as I stood up to hug her and fell into her arms as I had all my life. For the rest of the evening I shared with her my feelings for friends whom she knew that had been far more than friendship in my heart. I told her this wasn't something I wanted. That I had no idea how I got here. That most of all, I didn't want her to be disappointed in me.

I shed many tears that night, but Mama didn't. Maybe she did when she got in the car to drive home. Maybe she did with my dad when she got home. We didn't ever talk about it. But I'm thankful for her strength that night and for her willingness to care for me in that moment as best she could. I know now that she must have had her own feelings to express. Her gift of hospitality, though, allowed her to set her own feelings aside for the time being and care for her daughter. It would soon be time for me to care for her, but not then. Not the Mother's Day night in my apartment in Lubbock when I told Mama I was gay.

When Mama got home, she told Daddy as I had asked her to. Initially he was angry, but it was soon confirmed as anger at himself, believing another myth that Christians have believed for so long – that I was gay because of his parenting, because of our difficult relationship. I couldn't assure him that it wasn't, because at the time, I didn't know myself. It would be another decade before I would begin questioning those ideas about sexuality that we had all been conditioned to believe. But, like Mama, Daddy told me he loved me and would always love me.

I watched my parents minister to many people over my lifetime, but I never dreamed that I would one day be the recipient of their greatest hospitality. I never imagined myself the outcast who would be welcomed and embraced by my own parents. But I was, and their Christlike love made all the difference.

4

The Birth of CenterPeace

While I was working as general counsel for the Texas Senate Education Committee for the 2001 Texas legislative session, amid the busiest day of the session, I received a phone call. It was the last day to hear bills in committee, and we were working sixteen- and seventeen-hour days, so I wasn't able to answer the phone. Later I listened intently to the message on my answering machine and heard the voice of my favorite professor from college.

"Sally, this is Carley Dodd at Abilene Christian University, and I'd like to talk to you about the possibility of coming back to coach the debate team and teach a few classes in the communication department."

The rest of the day and night I pondered the thought of returning to teach at the university that had given me so much. It would be a chance to give back to a place that was beloved by me and my mom. Excitement built as I called Carley back. I knew that I would have to tell Carley everything. I had not yet come out to anyone but my counselor, my parents, and a few close friends. This was a critical time in my spiritual journey because I was already feeling the nudge from God to minister to other Christians who were experiencing attractions to the same sex. I would have to tell him about this dream I'd had now for a couple of years – of creating some type of ministry that would address faith and sexuality in a way that had never been available for me in my own pain.

I kept thinking of friends who had been rejected by their families because of their sexuality. Friends whose parents were church leaders. Friends who themselves were devoted to God, wanting to serve in ministry. Friends I had known since childhood, whom I knew to be precious souls, yet we never talked about the growing confusion inside each of us over our sexuality. What if there had been more conversation about our sexuality when we were young? What if those conversations had been initiated from a Christian perspective? What if there had been resources for us and our parents? What if our churches that had been an integral part of our lives hadn't been shrouded in fear of this topic, but had embraced it, and us, rather than perpetuating decades of secrecy and shame?

I realized the need for a ministry to address these concerns, but I was also terrified of what that would mean. It would mean that I would have to come out publicly, to help people in churches understand the truth about another myth that was deeply entrenched in Christians – that someone who is gay has rebelled against God. That certainly wasn't true about me. I had never turned my back on God. I had never stopped believing, going to church, praying, or reading Scripture. I did all those things. And many of my gay friends did, too. So, despite fears of sharing my story publicly, the last couple of years I had begun praying, "God, if this is what you want me to do, then give me an unquenchable zeal for this ministry. Give me courage and passion, so that I won't want to stop." And he did.

I knew that ACU's current administration might not be comfortable with my acknowledgment of experiencing attraction to the same sex. Even after learning of my traditional views on homosexuality, the administration might not want me there. Would ACU hire someone to teach on the faculty who admitted to being attracted to her own sex, even if she didn't identify as gay and sincerely believed it would be wrong to act on those sexual feelings? At the time, I was committed to living a single, celibate life. I knew I would not be able to work at the university unless they were on board with my creating a ministry to address faith and sexuality. So I drove to Abilene to share all this with Carley and see if it was worth applying for the position.

Carley's response was overwhelmingly kind, gracious, and most supportive, just as I expected. Wanting to be totally up front, we both agreed that the next step would be to seek out the department chair's opinion and go from there. Joe Cardot, chair of the communication department, also responded positively, and having no qualms about my being a part of his faculty, took the question to the dean of the College of Arts and Sciences, Colleen Durrington. Dean Durrington was agreeable and reported the situation to the provost, Dwayne VanRheenen, who took the news all the way to the university president at the time, Royce Money. When Dr. Money gave the okay for me to be officially considered, I began the interviewing process and within a couple of months I was moving to Abilene.

If there was ever any concern about hiring a woman attracted to other women, I never heard about it. I was always treated warmly and was included in the life of the ACU campus with no hesitation. Perhaps they would have been less receptive to hiring me had I held a viewpoint that affirmed same-sex relationships. But I never asked that question of any of them, so I can't know for sure. It was also a very different time in 2001, at least in the Christian world. The word "gay" still meant that a person was blatantly promiscuous and obviously rebelling against God. The phrase "same-sex attraction" was still relatively new in Christian circles. It fit my experience, though, and was less derogatory to me than being called "a homosexual." Looking back, what I know for certain is that I felt loved and embraced on the campus, fully included in my department, and happy to be back in the classroom, teaching at my alma mater.

Starting a ministry, while teaching at ACU, would require me to become more comfortable sharing my sexuality with others, first with loved ones, and later in public settings. Initially I was scared to death to tell anyone about my sexuality. But in 2003, I was invited to speak to five thousand students and faculty at ACU during chapel. It would be my first public disclosure. For two months prior to that talk, I was petrified. Whenever I would think about sharing this part of myself – this secret I had kept entirely to myself until the last few years – I felt like I was having a panic attack. I worried about what my students would think. Would they drop my classes? What would happen when their parents found out? Alumni? Not to mention my fellow faculty members? I feared everyone would look at me differently and treat me differently after I disclosed that I was attracted to women.

That morning, despite my fear, I felt increasingly determined the closer it got to 11 a.m. and the start of chapel. My mom and dad drove in from Wichita Falls and were seated in the front row in full support of me. The time came, and I walked up the steps of the rostrum and took my seat next to the other chapel participants. As I sat there talking to God in my head, trying to keep it together, I looked out into the black abyss of the crowd, and the only people I could recognize were my parents. I had sat in this coliseum so many times, for chapel when I was in school, for Sing Song, for Lectureship, and yet I had never seen Moody Coliseum from this angle. The lights in the audience were dimmed, with bright lights shining on the stage. When I walked to the podium, my legs shaking and my whole body quivering, all I could do in that moment, looking out at the crowd, was to say, "Wow." Then I proceeded to tell my story.

When I finished, I saw Jack Rich, vice president of finance at the time, stand up, applauding. From there, others stood and gave me a standing ovation. It was over. But it was just the beginning. That afternoon, students came by my office to talk, saying "me, too," and they emailed me for years after that, remembering that I was someone safe to talk to. After that chapel experience, I was even more convinced of the great need on our college campuses and in our churches to open this conversation about faith and sexuality.

A year later I asked trusted voices of experience in ministry to begin meeting once a month. Over the next year and a half, we planned every detail of putting a ministry together, including the selection of the name, CenterPeace. Why that name? I was at church one Sunday when my eyes rested upon the communion table. A bouquet of flowers was in the middle of the table, a centerpiece. I began playing with the word until I came up with "centerpeace" – thinking about the table and the purpose behind it. The name CenterPeace is founded on the truth that Jesus invites us all to the table, where he is the centerpiece, the very centerpiece of our existence. Without him at the center of our lives, we have no peace. Everybody gets to come to the table. Jesus does the inviting, not us. No one is excluded, no matter what their "table manners."

In 2006, CenterPeace was incorporated with the State of Texas and shortly thereafter gained nonprofit status as a §501(c)(3) organization. The same radical hospitality of Christ that was modeled for me by my parents and extended to me by them when I came out, became the core ethos of CenterPeace. Everyone was welcomed to the table, no matter where they were in their thinking regarding the morality of sexuality. For it's there at the table, where Christ is the head and we experience the loving embrace and fellowship with God through him and fellow believers, that we come to know what it means to be a disciple, a follower of Christ. Being cut off from the vine, excluded from the table, we soon forget, lose interest, and go our own way. But as recipients of the Lord's hospitality in inviting us to the table, we are constantly reminded of who we're called to be.

That hospitality began in small ways, inviting students into my home once a week. For ten years, students who were questioning their sexuality in one way or another came together to discover they were not alone. Drinking strawberry lemonade and eating chocolate-chip cookies fresh out of the oven and playing fetch with my dachshund, Chester, helped students to open up and share their feelings. The smell of cookies baking and a friendly dog created a relaxed atmosphere to share hard things. We started out reading books together, talking about what fit with our own experiences and what didn't. One summer we worked through the Psalms together, and another semester, the Gospel of John. We shared meals and watched movies. We became family to one another. As one student said, "This is more like a life group than the one I go to at church!"

Shortly after the student group started, I initiated a group for parents and family members in Abilene. Meeting in people's homes carries a certain power, so that's what we did, serving coffee and something sweet to eat every time we met. Just like the students, the parents responded positively to the hospitality and warmth of sitting on a couch in the living room, talking, drinking coffee, and occasionally reaching down to pet the dog.

Eventually CenterPeace began to offer workshops at individual churches, Christian universities, and conferences, helping church leaders better understand LGBTQ people and how to create a more Christlike response. Then spiritual formation retreats for LGBTQ people were added to the ministry effort. Those suffering in shame to the point of contemplating suicide, or who had left church entirely, were reminded of their belovedness. We also began hosting retreats for parents of LGBTQ children, realizing that whole families were in pain and had no place to talk about their feelings when a family member came out to them.

Over and over I witnessed the impact of Christlike hospitality, as church leaders and parents, even those with conservative views on sexuality, extended kindness and welcome. And that hospitality – or lack of it – can make the difference between life and death.

Tears were running down Mike's face as he came barreling down the outside aisle of the auditorium. It was 2008, and I had just come out to another audience of thousands of college students and faculty at Harding University in Searcy, Arkansas. When Mike walked over to me, he was visibly shaken. Through tears he thanked me and said my story was his story, too. Mike is gay and grew up in the church, but he'd never heard anybody talk about sexuality like I had, from a Christian viewpoint.

We went to lunch afterward with Cindi, the faculty member who was instrumental in my coming to Harding. She had been Mike's theater professor when he was a student at the university and had become his dear friend since his return to Arkansas. They reconnected when Mike started attending the church where Cindi and her husband, Dan, were leaders. But how Mike started going to their church is another story.

Mike had just returned to his roots of southeast Arkansas a few months before, and being poor and without a car, he walked everywhere in the small town of Searcy. One day the preacher from the Downtown Church of Christ, Matthew, was driving along and happened to see Mike walking. Matthew offered him a ride. Mike accepted, and he and Matthew started up a conversation. Soon, the rides and talks became more frequent, as Matthew would often see Mike out running errands for his work at a community theater in downtown Searcy.

As Mike began to open up about his life, Matthew invited him to drop by his office just to talk. Mike took him up on the offer, and slowly, over time, he began showing up at Sunday morning services at the Downtown Church. He reconnected with Cindi and Dan, who was a Bible professor at the university. Mike got involved in a Bible class and a small group, and extrovert that he was, Mike became acquainted with lots of folks in the congregation. Eventually, Mike shared his testimony to a packed auditorium one Sunday. The Downtown Church wasn't affirming, and still isn't, but they knew how to love and welcome Mike, and they did.

Several years before, Mike had left Searcy. He was asked to leave Harding University two months shy of graduating, after it was discovered he was in a same-sex relationship. Humiliated and without support from his family, Mike left home and ended up in Seattle, where he found a partner and worked as a drag queen in Capitol Hill, the largest gay district in the country at the time. Renowned in the LGBTQ community as "Miss Kimberly," Mike had mastered the art of performing in drag and sang to packed houses every night. Eventually, though, Mike developed a serious heart condition, hindering his work and the long-term sustainability he had hoped for in his relationship with his partner. Mike eventually returned home to Arkansas for a surgical procedure, which was followed by a lengthy recovery. When he returned, he was on his own, without family or community support.

The willingness of a stranger – a pastor – to stop and pick another stranger up off the street saved Mike, as he would later explain. Matthew's ride led him to experience the hospitality of a family and a church and more families. And in the midst of all that hospitality he was receiving, he began working to reconcile with his biological family.

Around this time, Cindi, Mike, and other dear souls they gathered along the way traveled to Abilene and experienced the hospitality of CenterPeace at our very first conference. Not only did Mike attend, but he read Scripture in one of the main sessions. He also sold T-shirts at the booth. At the conference, Mike made more friends from all over the country. And from then on, he helped with every event we sponsored, wanting to help others experience belonging in the same way he had. Mike often told me at our spiritual formation retreats that he wished we could live like that all the time. He wanted everyone to have their own cabin, all close enough together so if you didn't want to be alone, you didn't have to be. He and I often dreamed of what a community like that would look like.

Over the next couple of years, Mike was tremendous at making people feel welcome at CenterPeace events. I looked forward to his continued service involvement in the ministry. Unfortunately, that didn't happen. During the last few weeks of Mike's life, he experienced a tremendous amount of pain from his family's rejection of him. His stepmother had been hospitalized and was not doing well. Mike wanted to visit her but was rebuffed by his family every time he asked to do so. On the night Mike died he forwarded an email from his brother to several trusted CenterPeace friends, including me. The email made it clear that Mike was not welcome around his family.

Around six thirty the following morning, I received a phone call from Matthew, telling me that Mike's body was found next to a country road, on a curve, near where his grandparents were buried. I could see that exact spot in my mind as Matthew told me. Mike had taken me to that spot years before, to show me where he went to think and pray when he was upset about something. As soon as we hung up, I began making plans with CenterPeace friends to drive to Searcy and speak at Mike's funeral. The Downtown Church continued to show hospitality to Mike even in death, making all the funeral arrangements and taking care of all the funeral home expense, as his family would have nothing to do with it. In addition, the Downtown Church took care of Mike's house and all his belongings when his family said they didn't want any of it.

Several months later, we made arrangements to scatter Mike's ashes. Friends from Searcy, Abilene, and the Dallas/Fort Worth area gathered at the site of our spiritual formation retreats – at the place where Mike wanted to stay and live forever, and never have to be alone again. As people arrived, I noticed Mike's father and stepmother and one of his brothers getting out of their truck. During the months since the funeral, they seemed changed. Softened. I hugged them and told them how glad we were that they came. When I hugged Mike's dad, I told him how thankful I was that he'd raised Mike to know Jesus. And that he could rest assured Mike never forgot.

That day we shared a barbecue lunch like we had so many times in that place with Mike, laughing, talking with his family, telling "Mikey" stories. We looked at pictures that brought laughter and tears, we sang his favorite hymns together, and we walked through the pasture to the lake. Mike's best friend spoke, someone prayed, and silently we emptied Mike's ashes into the water. We let go of our balloons and watched the wind take them up until they disappeared into the sky, tiny ink blots of color in the clouds. We took our time walking back to our cars.

Before we departed, Mike's family came over to say goodbye. His father and stepmother thanked us for inviting them, and his brother, looking at me with Mike's eyes, said, "We always wanted to make things right with Mike. We just never knew how."

I remember the spot where I was standing in my living room the day I answered a call from Law Domasig. Law called to tell me about his son, David, "who thought he was gay but really wasn't." Law and his wife, Dawn, lived in Fort Worth at the time, but previously they had lived in Lubbock. They were both deeply upset when their oldest son came out to them. He was a student at Harding University, in Searcy, Arkansas, and they were both convinced that this was just a phase for him.

"He can't possibly be gay," Law told me. "I've known him all his life, and there's just no way he could be gay. He's just been brainwashed or something, gotten in with the wrong crowd, I don't know. But he can't be gay."

I listened as Law told me about how he and Dawn had raised all their children to be faithful Christians. I listened to Law express his fear of anything keeping his son from being right with God.

"He can't be homosexual and go to heaven," Law said. "The Bible is very clear about that."

I could tell Law was frustrated and noticed a growing agitation in his voice.

"That's what's so scary – he thinks this is okay! It's not okay!" Law said, growing more agitated. Then he fell quiet for a long while.

Finally he asked, "What do we do? Our youth minister said you would know what to do."

When their son first came out to them, Law and Dawn talked with the youth minister at their church, Will. Will and I knew each other and had visited more than once about working with LGBTQ teens and their parents. So when the Domasigs talked to him about their son, he put them in contact with me. But he also put them in touch with an elder at a church in Lubbock who was also the father of a gay son. Ben Cole understood where Law was much more than I could.

I began sharing my own story with Law. I told him how I, too, had been raised to believe that this was the worst possible thing that could happen and that I surely couldn't be gay. Praying fervently to God, asking him to remove those feelings, though, hadn't worked in the way I had hoped. I shared how my parents had never walked away from me, and how that had been the second greatest blessing of my life. The first being that they taught me about Jesus.

"Law, that's the most important thing you can do right now for your son. Just love him. Tell him again and again how much you love him and how proud you are of him," I said. "Reassure him that nothing will ever separate the two of you."

Law listened. And then he asked the same question: "But what do we do?"

That was the first of several conversations I had with Law. Law persisted in believing that his son would need to change his sexual orientation to be right with God, so we talked about that a lot. We talked about the fact that his son had not chosen to be gay. I explained that being gay was much more than sexual behavior; it was a way of relating to people and seeing oneself that goes far beyond mere sexual activity. We talked for hours over the phone. Sometimes it would be months between calls. And over time, I came to love this Filipino father, a second-generation American. We came to know each other and develop a friendship. The fact that this father was committed to understanding and reaching out to his son touched me deeply.

Meanwhile, I became friends with Dawn on Facebook, and when I moved to Dallas, they reached out to me again. When I announced a parent group meeting at my home, they drove all the way from Fort Worth, clear across the DFW metroplex, to attend. For the next few years, Law and Dawn were faithful participants in the parent group. They were still very traditional in their views about sexual morality, but they were just as adamant about staying connected to their son. Since our first conversation, their son's faith had begun to wane, ultimately leading him to a place where he wanted no more to do with the church. As Law and Dawn began to realize how much their son's feelings stemmed from hurt growing up in the church, hearing derogatory comments about people who are gay, they were intent on restoring their son's faith.

The Domasigs became one of the couples I could depend on to assist at our retreats. They would spend retreat weekends talking with moms and dads about their own experience and providing a safe place for parents to express their feelings and concerns. What came out most clearly when Law shared openly with groups of parents at our retreats was his love for his son, his commitment to stay connected to his children and love them as God does – unconditionally.

In private conversations and with our network of parents, Law and Dawn told us about their son's boyfriend and the very likely possibility that they would marry.

"I love my son and I always will," Law said in a slow, calm voice. "But I just can't support him in getting married. That's just wrong."

Most of the parents were quiet in the room, sipping their coffee and munching on the dessert one of them had baked that night. One of the dads whose son had come out to his family at age fifteen, Gil Vollmering, who was also an elder at his church, spoke up.

"I get that, Law," Gil said. "That's what I was raised to believe, too. Can I ask you something?"

"Sure," Law said, putting a bite of cake in his mouth.

"Let's say your son was dating a girl whom you didn't approve of or that you had concerns about. Maybe she wasn't a Christian. Maybe she wasn't a good spiritual influence on him. What would you do in that case?" Gil asked.

At this point Dawn chimed in: "Well, I think we would talk to him about our concerns. We would certainly ask questions."

"Yeah, I mean, we wouldn't hold back from saying something to him, especially if we hadn't talked to him about our concerns before," Law added.

Gil asked them, "Is there any chance that your son

doesn't know your concerns about him dating and marrying another man?"

Dawn chuckled, "Oh no. I'm pretty sure he knows!"

"Would you support your son in marrying a woman you didn't approve of, even after you'd talked to him and expressed your concerns?" Gil asked. "I mean, would you not participate in the engagement? Would you not go to the wedding?"

The room fell quiet. I could sense everyone in the room asking themselves the same questions. After a moment or two of silence, Law spoke up.

"I see what you're getting at, but it's different," Law said.

Gil grinned. "Really? How is it different?"

"Well, it just is."

Dawn looked at Law as she spoke. "We would go ahead and support him in a marriage to a woman, even if she wasn't a faithful Christian, because we would believe that, rather than turning away and shunning him, we could have greater influence in his life by supporting him. And ultimately, what matters most to us is that he is a Christian. Turning our backs on him at such an important time in his life, no matter what we thought of his decision, would not serve to draw him closer to God. In fact, it would push him further away."

"Yeah," Law continued. "And it's really inconsistent for us to be more concerned about the sex of the person he's dating or marrying, rather than the person's spiritual maturity and background."

"We haven't gotten to know this young man our son is dating. That's what we need to be focusing on, getting to know him and being involved in their lives," Dawn said. "The other young man's family is fully accepting of their relationship. What must our hesitance say to them?"

"I just don't know if I can go to a wedding like that," Law confessed.

Several months later the Domasigs' son wanted to bring his boyfriend home for a weekend. The parent group prayed the entire weekend for peace and calm for Law and Dawn and their family, for things to be "normal" between them and their son, and for them to extend a gracious welcome to his boyfriend. On Monday, while driving home from a meeting, I received a call from Law, telling me about the wonderful weekend they had. He told me about getting to know Andres, and how everyone seemed to be relaxed. And then Law shared a revelation.

"Before David and Andres got to our house, it just dawned on me that I didn't even know if Andres was a Christian or not," Law began. "I was so focused on the same-sex aspect of their relationship that I hadn't even thought to ask about the most important thing!"

Law chuckled and continued. "You know, I got to thinking, what if he's not a Christian? What if he's never known Jesus? What if he didn't grow up in a Christian home? Maybe this is the first time he's been around a family who is Christian."

"Yeah . . . ," I started to say before Law broke in again.

"So I'm thinking now," Law said excitedly. "We have a responsibility to welcome him as a stranger, to show hospitality to him, and to model Christ's kindness!"

I was beaming on the inside, because I knew this to be Law's heart all along.

"That's exactly right, Law," I assured him. "Either that, or he may need to see a totally different picture of Christianity than he's seen before. That's the way it is for so many people in the LGBTQ community. People have been so wounded by the churches they've wanted to be a part of that it's hard to not become bitter and resentful. It's only through sincerely extending God's unconditional love that the LGBTQ community will feel safe among Christians again."

"I hadn't ever thought about it that way, but we have an opportunity to live out the gospel," Law said. "And we can't turn away from that."

Not too long afterward, David and Andres announced their engagement. Law and Dawn and their two other children attended the wedding. By that time Dawn had read everything she could get her hands on about LGBTQ and had engaged in conversations with moms from all over. Law remained committed to a traditional sexual ethic, but not more than he was committed to loving and supporting his son. The son he loved now was the same son he loved before he learned this one more thing about him – that he was gay. Finding out that David was gay hadn't changed David at all. It simply meant that Law knew more about his son now, and over the last several years, he had learned even more about what it means to be LGBTQ.

Several months after David and Andres had married, I attended a community dinner at Law and Dawn's house. Law greeted me at the door with a big hug, calling me "Sister!" as he often did, and we walked into the living room where everyone was congregated. It was a cold night, and I could smell the aroma of soup and cornbread coming from the kitchen. Laughter and people visiting filled the room. The house was warm and cozy, perfect for greeting people who often felt left out. As I said hello to people and handed my coat to Law, my gaze fell on a photograph on a table in the most prominent place in the living room — a photograph of Law and Dawn with David and Andres at their recent wedding.

In the picture, Law is grinning from ear to ear.

Part 2

Interpreting Scripture

Do your best to present yourself to God as one approved, a worker who does not need to be ashamed and who correctly handles the word of truth.

(2 Tim. 2:15)

5

The Spirit of the Law

"*How you view Scripture in twenty-five years will not be the same as how you view Scripture today,*" my college professor calmly told the class, holding his Bible up over his head with one hand, turning from side to side as he spoke.

Did he just say what I think he said? My heart was racing. I was aghast at the thought.

When I was in my last year of graduate school, studying communication, I got special permission to take a class that traditionally had been offered only to men who were Bible majors planning to go into ministry. The class was advanced preaching. Very few courses in my degree focused on public speaking, but this was what I wanted to do with my degree. The professor granted me permission, and I became the first woman to ever take the class offered at the graduate level – one woman in a class of around thirty men.

On the first day, I was asked to stand up in front of my male peers and explain that I had no desire to seek employment in a church or go into full-time preaching anywhere, and that I simply wanted to take a course that was designed to help me improve my speaking skills. Most of the guys were friends of mine and very supportive of me. The class was especially fun when we were assigned to perform a wedding or a funeral. I filled in as the corpse for the funerals and the bride for the weddings. Technically, I've been married nine or ten times, but who's counting?

When I signed up for the class, I truly had no desire to work in pastoral ministry. That wasn't even a consideration, because it wasn't possible back in the mid-1980s in the Bible Belt, not in my church circles anyway. Plus, at the time, I still believed it would be wrong for me as a woman to work in a ministerial capacity on staff at a church. At no point during the class did those feelings change. I had been taught all my life that women served in the church differently than men, and while I might have seen the inconsistencies with which those standards were applied, I was not one to make waves. In fact, I agreed so strongly with the prohibition against women in public roles in the church that I turned down a campus ministry position my professor offered me after I finished my master's degree.

Despite my conservative views on women's ministry roles, I learned more in that semester preaching class than I did in any other course as an undergraduate and graduate student combined. It wasn't easy to pull an A in Dr. Mike Lewis's classes, sometimes even a B, but I liked the way he taught. I liked how he used the latest technology to teach us in ways that had never been used before, like the time we analyzed the organizational communication patterns in an old war movie from the 1970s called *Kelly's Heroes*. We gathered in small groups to watch the movie over and over on a brand-new beta video player, before the days of VCRs. But most of all, what I gained from the class was greater insight into presentation skills and Scripture, as well as bringing a message to life for listeners. I learned about structuring sermons using inductive versus deductive reasoning. I learned about exegesis. I began to believe I could be good at speaking to an audience.

But that one comment from Dr. Lewis – out of hours, days, months of instruction – stands out to me more than anything else I remember about the class: "*How you view Scripture in twenty-five years will not be the same as how you view Scripture today*."

At the time he said it, I disagreed vehemently. I might have been only twenty-two years old, but I knew for certain that what Scripture said didn't change. How could he have said such a thing? Didn't he know what Jesus said: "I am the same today, tomorrow, always"? Of course, that applies to Scripture because Jesus is the Word. I couldn't believe my professor said that.

I looked up to this teacher. When Dr. Lewis was first hired by Abilene Christian, I was a senior. I remember another professor introducing him to us as a former pastor of a local congregation who had also taught organizational communication at a major university in Florida. On top of that, he had done consulting for Disney. At the time, I contemplated a career in consulting too, so I listened to what this man had to say. The first time he complimented my work, I thought I had arrived. In a graduate communication theory class, after a three-hour written exam, he wrote "super job" on the top of my blue book and gave me full credit. And when I took the advanced preaching class, he told the pastor at my church, while they were playing golf, that I did a better job on the exegetical sermon assignment than any of the guys in the class. Wow, I thought. This man's opinions mattered to me, and while I tried no harder in his classes than I did in the others, I believe he saw something in me that I didn't yet see in myself.

Even still, his statement about Scripture alarmed me. One thing I've always loved about my Church of Christ heritage is our deep love for Scripture as the primary means of discernment. The vision of Alexander Campbell, our denomination's founder, started with a desire to call Christians back to our roots of Scripture. What this typically meant was an interpretive approach that pieced together different passages of the Bible on a particular topic to arrive at a conclusion (also known as "proof texting"). My faith tradition taught us "to speak where the Bible speaks, and to be silent where it's silent." We drew from Scripture which practices should be included in our worship services and which practices should not be. From the Bible we determined that prayer, singing, teaching, and sharing the Lord's Supper were included in the early church's worship and therefore should be included in our services as well. We paid close attention to how they were administered in the New Testament church, and sought to follow accordingly.

One of the most important of those practices is communion. When I was a kid, communion was served at my church in the same way, at the same time during the worship service, every week. There was no variation, no attempt to do anything in a novel way. Why? Because we had discerned that this way was *the* way communion was meant to be served. So, every Sunday men lined up on either side of the communion table that had "This Do in Remembrance of Me" engraved on it at the front of our church. Each week they stood with their hands folded in front of them, staring at the back wall with somber expressions on their faces, dressed in suits and ties (except for the teenaged boys on the ends who were still growing and didn't have suits that fit them).

The men sat in the front row of the auditorium for the first part of the worship service. If we had a well-practiced song leader, he would indicate when we were about to serve communion by introducing the next hymn as one "to prepare our minds for the Lord's Supper." Then, in four-part harmony, we would softly sing a hymn – something like "When My Love to Christ Grows Weak" or "Have Thine Own Way" or "Father, Hear the Prayer We Offer." Toward the end of the last verse, the men sitting in the front row would solemnly walk to the front of the auditorium and line up on either side of the communion table, facing the congregation.

After the song, a man walked to the podium and read the passage of Scripture recounting Jesus eating with his disciples the night before he died, or another passage from one of Paul's letters talking about how we are to "take" communion. Then the assigned leader prayed over the bread, and the men standing next to the table began passing the shiny silver trays of matzo crackers down to all the other men.

When all the trays had been passed down, the men headed down the aisles of the auditorium. I'm not exactly sure how they knew when to move, but they always "broke" at precisely the same time and began passing the trays down the rows of people. During communion, it was so quiet you could hear a pin drop, except for the occasional cough and crying baby or toddler screaming, "No, Mama, I'll be good!" as their mother dragged them out of the auditorium.

For as long as my mother was able to attend Sunday morning services, she would receive the tray with one hand and, with the other, pinch off the smallest piece of cracker she could manage. We attended a congregation where those trays were expected to serve hundreds of people, so she said she didn't ever want to take very much. Besides, the piece of cracker was a mere emblem. Enough to remind us of the Lord's body, sacrificed for us on the cross, Mama would say, but never intended to feed us. Sensible and frugal in many ways, Mama was a true daughter of the Great Depression.

As soon as everyone had been served "the bread," the men gathered at the back with the cracker trays, lined up on both aisles symmetrically (we took that verse to do "everything in decency and in order" very literally and believed it applied here), and marched in even rows back up to the front. The same man walked back to the podium and said a prayer for "the cup." Then the servers went through the same dance with trays of tiny little cups filled with grape juice. The men usually took only two trays, unless they had strong and ambidextrous hands and could handle three.

After I had been baptized, whenever I was sitting with my parents and not with the youth group, my dad would hold the tray for both Mama and me to get our little cups of juice and then we would all three drink at the same time. Back then, before the days of disposable plastic, the cups were made out of heavy glass, so they had to be washed after every use. Even before I was permitted to partake in the symbolic gesture that was communion, I knew this was a solemn time. It was a time to think about the sacrifice that Jesus had made for all of us. For that reason, I was taught, it was important to serve communion in the right way.

That's why one Sunday when my mom and dad and I were on vacation and visiting another church (as was our custom anytime we traveled out of town), when communion was served differently, we got up and walked out. Someone at the church had explained beforehand that they were going to do something different that morning while taking the Lord's Supper. He then directed everyone to form a circle around the perimeter of the auditorium. We did so. To my left a microphone had been placed on a stand, and as they started passing the tray of bread around the circle, a man and woman began singing a duet. My mom looked at my dad and whispered something to him. Seconds later, she was grabbing my wrist and we were out the door. I don't remember anything about that Sunday morning except the circle of people and a woman in a red dress singing.

At the age of ten, I understood why we left, namely, because communion was not being served in precisely the same way we were accustomed to having it served. If some aspect of the worship service was conducted differently, surely the new way was wrong. This was a Church of Christ, after all. Didn't they know that our people had consulted the Scriptures and determined the right way to perform this ritual, *years*, if not decades, ago? What, then, was another church – *another Church of Christ* – doing serving communion in a different way? Surely this church had gone off the rails. Didn't they know that nowhere in Scripture did it talk about people standing in a circle to partake of the

Lord's Supper? And the Bible surely doesn't mention anybody singing while communion is being served, particularly not two people singled out, who surely were doing that just to be seen! They must not have studied the Scriptures on communion very much, because even at ten years old, I knew all these reasons.

If something wasn't mentioned specifically in the Bible, then we didn't incorporate it into our way of doing things. Likewise, if we found a verse of Scripture that instructed how to do something, that's the way we tried to do it, to the exclusion of anything else. This way of reading the Bible also influenced our distinct practice of a cappella singing. The scriptural argument for not using instruments in worship within the Church of Christ has always been, first, that *singing* (not use of instruments) is directly commanded ("speaking to one another with psalms, hymns, and songs from the Spirit. Sing and make music from your heart to the Lord" [Eph. 5:19]). Second, in the New Testament passages that depict worship style and practices, *instruments* are never mentioned. That is, we made an argument from silence. Of course, I came to realize later that just because musical instruments aren't specifically mentioned in the New Testament doesn't mean that the early Christians didn't, in fact, use them. This is a prime example of how we followed Alexander Campbell's "speak where the Bible speaks, and be silent where the Bible is silent."

The fact that I still remember these stories and proof texts concerning communion and singing is evidence of how sincere I was in learning why we did the things we did, and why some things were prohibited. I was taught to "always be able to give an account" of whatever I believed, and I was able to do this at a very young age. But as I got older, I began to see that the reasoning I had once thought was so clear wasn't nearly so clear and compelling.

The first challenge to my beliefs about a cappella music was the use of a pitch pipe. Why was it okay to use a pitch pipe but not a harmonica, which is similar? Could a pitch pipe be considered a musical instrument? Technically, no, and furthermore, it wasn't used to accompany the singing of the song. But if the rule for prohibiting elements of worship was based strictly on what was and was not mentioned in Scripture as part of the New Testament church, then we shouldn't be using a pitch pipe, because it's never talked about in Scripture. Or, for that matter, a sound system. Or a hymnal. And that, of course, is the same argument some people used when we wanted to employ an overhead projector to show new songs on the screen. But if you follow this line of reasoning to its logical application and conclusion, we couldn't have water fountains or electricity or kitchens or . . . well, you see where this is going. To truly restore the New Testament church, we would need to start living in very primitive homes and then meeting for worship in our houses.

This is the way I was taught to reason through every aspect of worship, to determine what was commanded, what was permitted, what was prohibited. Those ideas were reinforced by my family, as illustrated by our leaving the church that circled up for communion in 1970. But when I was in college a decade later, I was confronted for the first time with the possibility of there being another way to partake of the Lord's Supper, and of it being okay. This may not seem like a big deal, but it was to me. My mind was opened to the possibility of difference – always accompanied by further study and examination of Scripture.

During my sophomore year at Abilene Christian, I took a night class in cultural anthropology. It was required for my degree and taught by a professor who had once been an overseas missionary, Dr. George Gurganus. We met down in the basement of the Administration Building, in a corner classroom that was dark and dank, especially at the back of the room where I sat next to the left wall. Dr. Gurganus wasn't dynamic or entertaining in the least, but one night he captured my complete attention.

The professor was sharing his experiences working with an indigenous tribe on the island of New Guinea, a remote area that didn't have access to global transportation, and thus no imported goods. While working with these people, helping to establish a church among the tribe, he naturally introduced them to the practice of sharing the Lord's Supper together. Dr. Gurganus taught them that communion consisted of unleavened bread (because that's how it's described in the New Testament). Similarly, Scripture says "fruit of the vine," so we've historically always used grape juice. Much to Dr. Gurganus's surprise, there were no grapevines in New Guinea. And nowhere on the island did they grow wheat. That meant that in New Guinea there was no Welch's grape juice, and no bread, leavened or unleavened. In teaching these people the meaning of communion, then, Dr. Gurganus had to reach beyond a wooden reading of Scripture. He explained to my class how he had reasoned through this, asking us to decide if this form of communion would be permissible based on Scripture.

The bread, representing Jesus's body, is considered the "staff of life," or food that sustains us. On the island of New Guinea,

Dr. Gurganus explained, sweet potatoes (at least at the time he was there) were considered the islanders' sustenance, and a substitute for bread. Just as bread has traditionally been served with meals in other parts of the world, sweet potatoes were served in New Guinea as a part of every meal.

In the same way, another fruit, similar to apples, grew in trees, and that was their equivalent to grapes, but it did not grow on a vine. So, the professor posed the question to my class: What would you do in that situation? What would you teach this remote tribe of people about the observance of the Lord's Supper? Would it be permissible to substitute emblems in a country that has no access to the ones specifically mentioned in Scripture? Would it be okay to use sweet potatoes and apple juice for communion?

I thought about that for a long time. I had been raised to see those passages of Scripture that talked about communion very literally and had never considered the possibility of bread and grape juice not being available to everybody on the planet throughout time. It became obvious to me that certainly, if something wasn't accessible, a substitute had to be permissible. Because, after all, communion was more about what – *who* – the bread and wine symbolized than about the actual food consumed, right? Furthermore, it was about our thoughts, about our hearts, about remembering Christ's death on the cross and making sure we carried no bitterness or grievances toward anyone into the sharing of that meal together. Wasn't it? A deeper, more meaningful reading of Scripture would say so. The spirit of the law would say so. Plenty of passages of Scripture indicate this. Simply put, it's not about the food, but the heart of the person partaking. Before the three-hour class had ended that night, I had experienced the first "crack" in my universe, realizing that something I had always believed to be so certain and unchanging had now shifted. And at least one thing in my world was a little less black and white.

This was just the beginning, but Dr. Mike Lewis, whom I quoted at the beginning of this chapter, was right. In the next twenty-five years, I would come to interpret Scripture differently. And believe in its relevance for my life all the more today.

6

What's in a Translation?

By the time I left graduate school in 1985, I knew the Brown Library on the campus of my alma mater, Abilene Christian University, like the back of my hand. Just to my right after entering the library were the card catalogues and the desks full of references to periodicals. I was well acquainted with the *Reader's Guide to Periodic Literature*, and I had worked out a very methodical system to make sure I didn't miss the most recent information, which required me to check all the monthly updates. I even knew where all the microfiche were kept, and I could find them in the categorized drawers and load them onto the readers. The world was my oyster in this space. I could learn anything and everything that was available at the time in this library. So quiet and serene, the library was a safe place for me – I knew my way around so well. Catching a whiff of the familiar aroma when I came in put me at ease. Everything I needed to do research in my field was accessible, and I could find it with my eyes closed in that library. That is, in 1985 I could find it.

When I came back to Abilene Christian University in 2001 as assistant professor of communication, the library looked quite different. The main floor had been totally renovated into a commons area that had only one section of stacks. Books had been moved to other floors of the library. Where books formerly filled rows there stood a copy center, a writing center, computer kiosks, and most important, a Starbucks café with plenty of seating.

All the card catalogue and reference materials were now digitized, accessible to all students and faculty on our online network. Now I could consult articles from journals that the Brown Library didn't carry – in a matter of seconds. And there on my computer screen, right in front of me, I could cut and paste information and source material in no time. I thought it was amazing! There was no end to what I could find.

But despite the benefits of digitization, it was all still new to me, and I often struggled to find what I wanted. Many times I wished I could just go find the paperback copies of the *Reader's Guide* and look up what I wanted, like I used to do. I had spent over a decade learning that old system, starting when I was just a kid, and that's the method of research that felt most natural to me. There was no denying, though, that this newfangled system was a gateway to information far beyond what I'd previously been able to access.

Thankfully, Starbucks helped me to adjust to the library makeover. From the minute I opened the door to the library, the undeniable aroma of Starbucks coffee wafted over me. The coffee shop fostered a whole new ambience. For starters, everybody was talking. Everywhere I looked, conversations were happening, from the computer stations to the booths in the corner by Starbucks. People were sitting in big soft chairs and couches, sipping lattes and talking. It was a new day. Never had I been in a school library where there was so much activity. And noise. But much of it, I came to realize, was related to learning. Students were studying and working on assignments. Professors were meeting with students in groups and interacting in ways I didn't get to experience when I was in school. The library was obviously different. But for a variety of reasons, it was good.

As a teacher, I came to utilize this space for a lot of meetings with fellow faculty members. In the spring of 2009, I had coffee in the library with a new faculty member in the Bible department. I had invited him to talk about a breakout session that I wanted him to teach at an upcoming CenterPeace conference. The conference was to be the first to ever discuss faith and sexuality in the Church of Christ and was set for September of 2009. My colleague was young, energetic, and bright, and had already expressed interest in helping with the conference. I envisioned him teaching something pertaining to Scripture, since the New Testament was his area of specialty. Like so many meetings that I planned back in those days, I came with an agenda in my head. When we sat down, I knew we would simply talk about what he would present at the conference. Or so I thought.

As it was, we talked about something entirely different. It turned out to be a pivotal conversation that expanded my understanding of biblical interpretation. In fact, I didn't realize how much I didn't know until it smacked me square in the face.

My colleague came to Abilene Christian from the University of Chicago. Our paths had crossed a little on campus, but I still didn't know him well. We went to church together, though, and he had expressed support for my work with CenterPeace. Given his background and training in New Testament, I was anxious to visit with him and see what he might be willing to present at the conference regarding the passages of Scripture that specifically addressed same-sex relationships. He arrived shortly after I did, and we quickly got in the Starbucks line to order coffee. Before we even sat down at a table, I could sense he was eager to show me something. We settled ourselves at the table and placed our belongings in the extra chairs. He quickly began rummaging around in his bag of books and papers, pulling out a stapled set of papers and placing them face down in front of him.

"Sally, how familiar are you with the ways language has changed in Scripture?" My colleague placed his arm on the table, leaned over slightly and propped his head up with his right hand, steadied his gaze on me with a grin, and waited for my answer. Well, I knew that my most recent Bible, a New Living Translation, was different from my previous New International Version. Before that, my *Harper Study Bible* from college days – a Revised Standard Version of the Bible – contained different language than the NIV. And they all read a bit differently from my very first Bible, the King James Version.

"Sure, I know it's changed a little in my lifetime," I responded.

"Yes," he agreed, "and it started changing long before you were born."

Slowly he turned over the stapled set of papers in front of him and gently pushed them toward me so I could see what was written on the first page. There were six pages in all, single spaced, with typing on the front and back of each page.

"You're familiar with these two particular verses people

cite in reference to homosexuality, aren't you?" My colleague pointed to the citation column. "1 Corinthians 6:9 and 1 Timothy 1:10?"

"Yes, of course," I said.

"Have you ever looked at the original language in those two verses?" he asked. Before I could answer no, he began writing in pencil at the top of the page where I could see more easily.

"These letters to the church at Corinth and to Timothy include a Greek term Paul seems to have coined: *arsenokoitēs*," he explained. "What has most recently been translated in many English Bibles as 'homosexual' or 'homosexuality' is actually two different words in the Greek that Paul combined to create a compound word."

At the top of the page he had scribbled *arsēn* followed by a plus sign and *koitē*. My colleague told me the first word meant male and the second word meant bed. Put together, the words were literally translated "male-bedder." He continued, "We don't really know what Paul had in mind, since this is the first time this particular compound term is ever used. The word originated with Paul, so without any more context or further usage, we can't be certain of what Paul was trying to say."

This wasn't the first time I'd heard this explanation. While I hadn't read gay-affirming theology extensively, I was familiar with the argument that we don't know for sure if these verses refer to committed same-sex relationships. I didn't find it persuasive. Even if the Greek term was ambiguous here, other places in Scripture clearly prohibited same-sex relationships. That's enough for me, I thought.

But then he started showing me the rest of the page. "Every one of these entries," he began, "shows a different translation of *arsenokoitēs*, starting with the Wycliffe version, the first English translation of the Bible."

I started reading down the list of translations. Finishing the first page, I turned to the second, and noticed that it, too, was filled with translations listed chronologically on the back of the first page. In total, he had compiled twelve pages of different English translations of *arsenokoitēs* from over hundreds of years. Toward the end of the handout, I finally reached more contemporary versions of the Bible I recognized. To my surprise, I noticed *arsenokoitēs* had only been translated "homosexual" and "homosexuality" within my lifetime. Prior to the mid-1900s, these words had not been used in English Bibles. Wording from earlier translations often conveyed a different, more ambiguous meaning of *arsenokoitēs*. For example, for 1 Corinthians 6:9:

› Tyndale (1534): "abusars of them selves with the mankynde"
› King James (1611): "abusers of themselves with mankinde"
› American Standard (1900): "abusers of themselves with men"
› New American Standard (1963): "homosexuals"
› New International (1984): "homosexual offenders"[1]
› New Living (2004): "homosexuals"
› English Standard (2007): "men who practice homosexuality"

I realized right then that my conversation with him was going in a much different direction than I had expected when we first sat down. For the next hour or so, he explained how the common interpretation of 1 Corinthians 6:9 and 1 Timothy 1:10 as prohibitions against *all* same-sex relationships might not be what Paul meant in his context. The question is, *What kind* of male sexual activity did Paul have in mind? I kept looking at the translations that had been used down through history that were different from what I thought the Bible had always said. The translations varied. In fact, some years after my meeting with him, I discovered that Martin Luther's original German Bible (1534) has the translation *knabenschander*, meaning molester of boys, a translation that more accurately reflects the pederasty Paul the apostle would have observed in his time.[2]

Prior to the very recent change to "homosexual," most translations seem to indicate abusive contexts, not loving relationships characterized by lifelong covenant. If the plain meaning of *arsenokoitēs* was so obvious, why the different translations? My mind was racing. I had no idea what to do with this new information. I had no reason to distrust my colleague. He was a Bible professor, and he'd been vetted and hired by my alma mater. My mother's alma mater. If there was a place I trusted to teach me about Scripture, surely it was this place. And besides all that, these various translations were accessible to me right where I was, in Brown Library. Just a few feet away were volumes of biblical scholarship and copies of all those translations. I could check for myself and see with my own eyes if the things he was telling me were true.

And with that, I felt another crack in the tectonic plate that was my world. It was the loudest crack yet.

I had contemplated the nature of Scripture before. In college, Dr. Gurganus helped me to see the spirit, and not just the letter, of the law. And when I was in high school, I had wondered about inspiration, given that Scripture was copied by scribes over and over before there was any such thing as a printing press. It made me curious as to how we could be sure – absolutely certain – that what God wanted us to have in Scripture from the beginning was the same thing recorded in my black leather King James Version of the Bible thousands of years later. In fact, I was so curious that by my senior year of high school, I chose the history of the King James Bible as the topic of my largest research assignment. Eventually I came to a place of accepting what I had always believed to be true: whatever God wanted me to know from Scripture, I could know. Only an unfair God would require something of me, and then have the only source from which I could learn that requirement be distorted. And I didn't believe in an unfair God.

But this new tectonic crack was different. My conversation with my colleague took my learning to a new level. What was I supposed to do with this new information? The issue was not just the scribal copying process, but that the original language was translated into different words or phrases over centuries. How could I know for sure what was meant in the first place? If translations had changed that many times, how could I understand what a biblical passage was really trying to convey? If the meaning was plain, why didn't all the translations agree? And if this was true for just these verses in 1 Corinthians 6 and 1 Timothy 1, in how many other places in Scripture had this happened? How could I be certain of anything I read in Scripture?

My world slowly turned upside down. The core of what I had

been taught all my life to be true and unshakeable had just had the guts shaken out of it. This was more than just a word or phrase being translated differently. This was about whether or not I could trust anything in the Bible. At that moment I didn't know that I could. If I couldn't trust this book that had formed the foundation of my world, what was I to do?

For the next few years, I wrestled with what to believe. I was angry with God, and I made no pretense of hiding my anger from him. I felt hurt and embarrassed, as though I had been duped. Yet, despite my inner turmoil, I began to realize I didn't feel distant from him; I felt closer. So much so that eventually I found the words of Peter – when Jesus asked if the disciples wanted to leave him – coming out of my mouth, "Lord, to whom shall we go? You have the words of eternal life" (John 6:68).

During this time in my life, I lived in a world that breathed Scripture. I was teaching at a Christian university, surrounded by people who had also given their lives to the teachings found in Scripture. What would happen if I claimed I had doubts about the Bible – about believing in God – about believing anything in Scripture? Would my world crumble? Fortunately, I worked among some of the dearest people on this earth. I taught alongside professors who had taught me at the beginning of their careers and who exemplified Christ every day. With those I was closest to, I was safe to confess my doubts. They met me for coffee. I talked, they listened. I didn't have to process what was happening alone.

7

Embracing Mystery

My new wrestling with Scripture was one factor that sparked a midlife crisis in me at forty-five years of age, give or take a few years. My way of coping could have been much worse – all I did was search Craigslist for a drum kit. Ever since I was in high school, I've wanted to play the drums, probably because I adored Karen Carpenter, and she was a drummer. Girl drummers were hard to come by when I was growing up. When my band director explained one morning during practice that we were short on percussionists and asked if any of us had an interest in learning to play, I was ecstatic. But back at home, Mama dashed my excitement, saying drums would be too loud, even in the garage. Being a compliant child, I stuck with the clarinet. Yet that dream of beating the tar out of drums never went away.

On Craigslist, I located a beautiful set previously owned by the teenage son of a missionary family that had returned overseas. They couldn't take the drums with them, so they left the set with friends of mine who lived a few blocks away. My adolescent dream of becoming a drummer was just up the street, so I got in my car as fast as I could and drove over to the house. After loading all the pieces into my Toyota – drums, "trees," hi-hat, and crash cymbals – I eagerly delivered them to their new home in my garage.

Over the next few weeks, I found YouTube videos that taught me the basics. Eventually I could keep a beat. A friend let me borrow a small sound system so I could play along with songs on my iPhone playlist. One of my favorites was Monty Python's "Always Live on the Bright Side of Life." It had a slow enough tempo that I could keep my hands and feet working at the same time and still feel like I was playing a real song. I'd sit out in the garage for hours, beating the living daylights out of those drums, blasting the music of my adolescence, and working out a lot of stress in the process.

I never intended to play the drums outside of the four walls of my garage. But a friend of mine happened to be leading worship at a small church on Wednesday nights, and she asked me to play. I was both exhilarated and mortified, but it didn't take much coaxing for me to agree. Playing with real-live musicians is a lot different than drumming along with an Eagles or Beatles recording. I rediscovered my love of playing with other people and being a part of a group that was creating music. I hadn't done that since my days in marching band in college, but it all came back to me – the thrill of creating a beat and a sound that moved people, the goose bumps that rose up on my arms when we all came together just right, the emotional swell that grew out of the music itself. It was magical to be part of something like that.

Eventually, word got around that I could keep a beat, and I was invited to be the drummer for a praise band at Freedom

Fellowship, another local church. They were desperate enough to ask me to join them on Wednesday nights, and the audience was gracious enough to let me play. We were a ragtag crew, but most of the time we sounded pretty good. Michael, the leader, played keyboard; Lucas played acoustic guitar; and Elizabeth sang lead soprano. Herb, a Vietnam vet with a gravelly voice who had smoked more than his share of cigarettes, accompanied on bass. Very quickly I came to love these guys.

At first, I saw myself as helping out a praise band team that needed me, while having some fun. What I didn't realize was how much Freedom Fellowship would come to impact my spiritual life. In the few years that I spent at Freedom, I grew spiritually in ways that I had never experienced before – not from six years at a Christian university or a lifetime in Bible classes and listening to sermons or attending spiritual retreats. I recovered my roots, my spiritual heritage of extending hospitality to those who have been disenfranchised.

Freedom was a church plant started by my home church, the Highland Church of Christ, in Abilene, Texas. Highland had always had a heart for ministry in the neighborhood, and Freedom was an extension of that. Highland bought an old, run-down church building constructed early in the twentieth century; it was located in one of the poorest parts of town, just south of the railroad tracks that separate the north and south sides of Abilene. Highland's community minister and his wife, Joe and Becky Almanza, were critical to the success of the new little church. They invested in people, all kinds of people, never turning anyone away.

A former drug kingpin whose family was one of the largest dealers in the Southwest, Joe had become a Christian while serving a prison sentence. When he was released, he traveled the country sharing how Christ had transformed his life. No one was too hardened, too intimidating for Joe. He knew the system, the language, the culture of the streets, and he was determined to offer the One who had changed his life to anyone he came in contact with. Together with a handful of leaders from Highland, Joe began to grow this new church among the poorest of the poor in Abilene.

Members of Freedom Fellowship walked the neighborhood, asking residents how we could pray for them and inviting them to meals and services on Wednesday nights. During the week, Narcotics Anonymous and Alcoholics Anonymous, as well as Bible studies, met in the building, filling up every night of the week. In time, some of the members created a community garden in an empty lot across the street from the church and began growing all kinds of vegetables, allowing anyone in need in the neighborhood to harvest them. On Wednesday nights, a meal was served, followed by a time of worship and praise, and some of the best teaching I heard all week.

The first night I attended Freedom, Paul Mathis got up and shared his battle with alcohol while serving as pastor in New England. His wife, Shawna, and their three children sat in the audience. You could have heard a pin drop, people were so attentive. Paul was speaking to people where they were at, people whose lives had been wrecked by addictions of all kinds. The auditorium was packed, making the hot summer night even more unbearable. What little air conditioning the old building had didn't work well, so the ceiling fans up in the highest part of the auditorium were going full blast. Still, it was hot and a stench filled the air, unlike anything I've ever experienced. Eventually I would come to accept this aroma of body odor and mothballs, bad breath from decaying teeth, and the mustiness of an old building. But that first night, the smell startled me, and so did some of the people I met.

Like Charles, the tambourine man who sat in the very front row.

Almost always dressed in a T-shirt and red suspenders holding up Bermuda shorts, Charles fortunately sat in the front row on the opposite side of the auditorium from where the praise band was set up. I say fortunately because he had no rhythm. Charles loved to play along with the band, yet he was always just a millisecond offbeat. Trying to play the drums with Charles in the audience, well, let's just say it was frustrating. But Charles and I became friends, and he never knew his timing was any different from mine.

Many of our friends at Freedom haven't finished high school, let alone gone to college. Many have learning disabilities that profoundly limit their ability to process difficult concepts. Many are not able to sit quietly and listen. Instead, they raise their hands excitedly, shouting, "Oh, I know!" Sometimes they don't raise their hands and wait to be called on but just blurt out an obvious answer.

Anthony was one of the church members with cognitive challenges that I came to know. He sauntered in quietly after the meal had been served and sat down in one of the pews about halfway back in the auditorium, directly in front of the band. Anthony was tall and slender with delicate features and a bit of gray at the hairline above his forehead. He always had a somber expression on his face, but he would smile and his eyes would light up when I talked with him. The first few times I talked with Anthony, I thought I was experiencing hearing loss. He talked so softly that I couldn't hear what he was saying, and what I did manage to hear, I couldn't understand.

It was difficult at first to try and carry on any semblance of conversation with Anthony. Most of what I could make out was gibberish or stories about having a job at Chase Manhattan Bank or being in charge of a chemists' lab. He lived on the streets when he wasn't in some type of shelter or rehabilitation program for the lifetime of drug use that had severely limited his ability to function. Living on the streets means you don't often have the chance to bathe or brush your teeth or wear clean clothes. When I sat next to Anthony, I was always overcome with the odor that emanated from him, especially when he moved or spoke. But under the layers of unwashed clothes, mostly garments that would've been worn by women, was a heart deeply in love with Jesus.

One night I noticed that Anthony had the Bible that he always brought with him opened to a certain page. He kept stroking the page lovingly, his long, thin fingers tracing over a picture of Jesus sitting with a group of children next to a tall palm tree. I asked Anthony about the image. Fidgeting in the pew, he turned toward me and began telling me about the picture.

"That's me right there," Anthony told me, pointing to the picture of the dark-complexioned youth sitting next to Jesus. "This picture was taken when we lived in Turkey. My dad was in the service, and Jesus came to visit us."

It was a picture often used in Sunday school classes to illustrate the gospel story of Jesus welcoming little children. But to Anthony it was real, more like a photograph capturing a memory of an actual event in his younger life. It illustrated his own personal encounter with Jesus. I wasn't about to counter that. So, we sat for a long while and talked about what it was like to spend an afternoon in Turkey with Jesus. Sometimes we lapsed into silence, Anthony smiling and occasionally patting the picture of the dark-skinned boy listening to Jesus. I smiled, too, wiping tears from my cheeks with one hand, my other arm cupped around Anthony's shoulders, draped with a worn and tattered pale pink women's sweater.

The folks at Freedom began to impact me in ways I never expected. At first, I was cynical, a cynicism picked up from absorbing society's derogatory comments about freeloaders and people just looking for a handout. That influenced my assessment of the Freedom members' attendance. *They're only coming for the food*, I thought. *A free meal*. But no one was obliged to stay once they had eaten. Everyone was free to leave once the meal had been served. Yet people stayed. And some people came who hadn't attended the meal.

Amid the souls I encountered at Freedom Fellowship God reminded me of some truths I had lost along the way. He reminded me of the "DNA of hospitality," which was ingrained in me but had been squelched by a culture of prosperity, by opportunities of education and financial assistance from parents early on in my young adult life that I had come to take for granted. I came to Freedom to play drums, and it was in that context, during those songs of praise, that I witnessed God working most powerfully.

When I first started playing with the praise band at Freedom, I was concerned with my drumming. Enough people from Highland were sitting in the audience that I cared more about how I sounded on the drums than about the people who had come to sing praise to God. And I never really got very good, but after a while it didn't matter. It didn't matter to this church how good I was. All that mattered was that I cared enough about God and them to show up. The more I realized that, the more God was able to show me in that place.

As I became more comfortable with my drumming, I began to look out into the crowd of people huddled in our worn building week after week. For the first time in my life, playing the drums enabled me to see people out in the audience singing. It was an angle I'd never witnessed before. Now I could watch the church praising God, and at Freedom, this was a sight to behold. In this group of ragamuffins who had been sidelined in our society, I saw the face of Jesus in each of theirs. In Charles playing his tambourine with the exuberance of a child. In Beth wearing her tiara, dancing with scarves in the front corner of the building with arms raised as high as her fingertips would allow. Some sang at the highest volume with little if any awareness of key or pitch. Some remained seated, swaying back and forth to the music, never making a sound.

It was a Wednesday night sometime after my meeting with my colleague in the library, and I was still trying to process what I learned about the Bible and translations. I still didn't have the answers I was looking for. I still didn't understand why some people wanted to act like the Bible was so easy to understand when it wasn't. More than that, if Scripture is *the* way — the only way – to know God, as I was raised to believe, what chance did I, let alone those at Freedom Fellowship, have if we can't fully understand it? These were the questions rumbling around in my head and heart as I picked up my drumsticks and situated myself on my stool, left foot on the hi-hat, right foot on the pedal of the bass drum, ready to pump out one, two, one two three four!

We often played a fast tune to draw everyone in from the meal in the kitchen and from the steps outside the front door. This part of the service was always one of my favorite moments, because of the fast pace, but also because I got to watch as friends sauntered in and took their seats in the pews. Sometimes they would wave hello to me and the other members of the band, and with my hands and feet occupied, all I could do was nod my head at them and grin.

I soon gave up on trying to choke back my tears from watching some of the most sincere worship I had seen. What I was now witnessing was very different from the stoic forms of worship I'd grown up with, where there was no movement nor hands raised, and facial expressions that hardly represented the freedom and hope about which we sang. These faces praising God just a few feet in front of me glistened with tears, and their hands stretched to the rafters, as far as they could reach. They sang with such exuberance that it was hard to remember the dire circumstances in which many of the congregation lived. Poverty, addiction, mental illness. Even in the midst of all that misfortune and pain, they cried out to God with thanksgiving – in the place where joy and sorrow meet.

One night when I first started playing the drums at Freedom, I looked down at my hands, at the two rings I had on, and at the watch I was wearing on my wrist. I began to think about the clothes I was wearing, about where they came from and how much they cost. I thought about the brand-new car I drove and the two-thousand-plus-square-foot house I lived in at the time with a dog, in a nice neighborhood where I'd never heard gunshots or raised voices. Suddenly I began to think about my roots, about all the opportunities I'd had because of my parents' sacrifices, and the sacrifices of their parents before them. The education they had made possible for me and an absence of debt as I entered adulthood, something that's virtually unheard of with the cost of a college education these days. I pondered the health care I'd had access to all my life, thanks to my parents, and recalled early memories of vaccinations and trips to the dentist.

My parents were not wealthy, but we weren't poor. Not when I looked out into the faces of Freedom. I didn't know anything about being poor, let alone living in poverty and what it does to a person's soul. For all but the first seventeen years of my life, I had lived in this city and never realized the depths of poverty and need within a ten-minute drive from my house. These were precious people whose lives had taken a significantly different turn from mine, solely because of the environment in which they were raised, physical and cognitive challenges that were not a result of their making, or a combination of both. I began to appreciate the needs of the people at Freedom. I began to see how much more difficult life was for those who hadn't had the same advantages I had, solely because of where and to whom they were born. No wonder their worship and praise to God looked different from mine. They were desperately reliant on God for everything, and grateful in the same breath.

Meanwhile I was going round and round with God, the insights from my conversation with him rattling in my brain. If the only way I can know God is through reading Scripture that is supposed to be unchanging and yet is clearly subject to different interpretations and translations, how can I ever come to know God?

"Why, God, if this is the way we come to know you, did you make it so difficult?" I asked. I kept pleading with him: "I want to know you, I truly do, and I want to understand what you want for my life, but I don't always understand your Word."

All my life I had heard that we can know what Scripture means through its "plain meaning." The Bible is very clear, I was always told. But at this point in my life, I felt like screaming, "No, it's not!" Many parts of Scripture are not clear. And as arrogant as this sounds, if I can't understand it, what chance do the people at Freedom Fellowship have? Only by the good fortune of being born into a family that valued education and provided for me, do I have undergraduate, graduate, and postgraduate degrees. Yet I still don't fully understand the Bible.

It was a Wednesday night in the midst of all this inner turmoil that I began to find resolution. I was playing drums, as usual, looking out into the faces of the worshipers. As I watched them and listened to their voices raised up to God in praise, I heard God speak in what theater buffs would call an "aside" moment. It was as though he were taking me aside to explain something to me, not only about the people I had come to love in this place but about something even bigger. Something about my view of Scripture, and how we come to know God.

In that moment I came to realize that God is much bigger

than the very limited version of God I grew up with. While he is certainly in the pages of Scripture, he is so far beyond the parameters of a book. He can be met in the stories of Abraham, Isaac, Jacob, and Moses, and in the letters of Paul. He is best known in the person of Jesus, but he is not confined to the gospel narratives. God is revealed in the birds of the air and the leaves of the trees. God dwells in the sacredness of cathedrals and in the desperation of brothels. He is in the face of my worst enemy and in the cry of a newborn baby. And those who seek him will surely find him, in all those places and so many more.

I heard him say, "No, Sally, you don't have to worry about your friends at Freedom not being able to know me because of their learning disabilities. And you don't have to worry that even with all your education you still have trouble understanding me. It's your heart I'm most concerned with, and your heart can meet me anywhere. I'm not only accessible to people through the Bible. Truth is, I am wherever people seek me."

I didn't hear God say those things audibly. But I heard from God that night. I was overcome with relief and began to cry. Suddenly, one of my drumsticks fell out of my hand and dropped to the floor. Startled, I reached down to pick it up, half laughing at myself, half overcome with an overwhelming sense of peace and joy. I believe with all my heart that the Holy Spirit expanded my view of how we come to recognize and learn about God in that moment – a moment that had been years in the making. I finally grasped that our knowledge and awareness of God and what he is like are not limited to the ability to understand the words on a page or the meaning behind each one. God is bigger.

God is bigger, Sally.

God is bigger than my ability to comprehend.

God is mystery.

And that's where faith comes in.

That night I went home with a peace I hadn't experienced in a long while. A peace that allowed me to believe in a God that I couldn't possibly fully understand. But that wasn't the point. The book didn't say, "I will have mercy on those who understand." God says in that book and in so many other ways, "I will have mercy on whom I have mercy" (Rom. 9:15). Over the next few months and years, I grew more comfortable with the truth that I will never fully grasp God. That truth has not doused my curiosity about him in the least. In fact, being freed from the insatiable need for certainty about my beliefs has given me greater certainty in the three things I know about God.

God is God and I am not.

Jesus is the most accurate description of God.

God loves me and my friends at Freedom Fellowship without condition and without end.

8

Overcoming Fear to Find Truth

While teaching at Abilene Christian University, I hosted a group of students who identified as gay or were questioning their sexuality. We met in my home once a week for ten years. Sometimes we spent the whole evening talking about a situation that one of the students was concerned over, like coming out to parents. Sometimes we ordered pizza and watched a movie. We shared tears together, but also a lot of laughter, usually over a plate of cookies. I was moved by the way they helped each other walk through challenges. I also learned a lot from them that I wouldn't have come to know any other way. My students were the ones who told me about Justin Lee for the first time, long before his best-selling book *Torn* was released.

"Justin's this gay Christian guy who started an online discussion group for people like us, you know, who are gay and don't know what to do with their faith," said Daniel.

"He calls himself a gay Christian?" I asked, as I placed the last piece of cookie dough on the baking sheet. "Why isn't he just a Christian who happens to be gay?"

"Well, I call myself a gay Christian," Erin piped in, "because the most important thing about me is that I'm a Christian. Gay just describes me, kinda like an adjective. Plus, it's a lot easier to say than 'I'm a Christian who's gay.'"

The English teacher in me thought about that for a second. Huh. You know, that's exactly right, I thought. "Okay, I get that. But why does he have to mention his sexual orientation at all?"

One of the veteran members of the group spoke up at that point. "Sally, I think a lot of it is because for so long being gay has been so shameful that there's now a specific move to identify as gay publicly to overcome all the negative stereotypes. Maybe it's just a generational difference in language. What did 'gay' mean when you were growing up?" he asked.

The students snickered, knowing I was about to go into my old person's voice. "Back in my day," I said in a voice closely resembling those two old men from *The Muppets Show* who always sat in the box seats at the theater, "if someone was 'gay,' it meant that they were extremely promiscuous, rebellious, and they had turned completely away from God." I added, "That's why I've always referred to myself as experiencing same-sex attraction rather than taking on a gay identity, because I wasn't like that at all. Calling somebody 'gay' back in my heyday of the 1970s was an insult. If you were a Christian, it was something you could never socially recover from."

"Yeah, I think the word 'gay' has changed quite a bit in how people use it today," the veteran student explained. "It simply refers to your sexual orientation and doesn't mean anything necessarily about your sexual behavior."

Several more students had arrived and were congregating around the counter that separated my kitchen from the living room. One student was pouring the last of the strawberry lemonade, and another was taking the mix down from the cabinet, preparing to make another pitcher. I tucked this new information away and returned to the issue of Justin Lee.

"He thinks same-sex relationships are okay, doesn't he?" I asked, taking the baked cookies out of the oven. I hoped my voice didn't betray my concern. The student group welcomed everyone, regardless of their theology on sexuality, but I still held a traditionalist view.

"Well, yeah, he does, but he respects that some people feel called to celibacy, and he doesn't leave them out," Daniel said. "He's got this chat room online, and he actually responds to the people who are on there."

Grabbing a handful of cookies, another student broke in. "Yeah, and you oughta see how many people are following him. Justin is the real deal. I heard him speak at my old church back home, and he's a really good guy," Stephen said, with all the seriousness he could muster in his voice. "I was in a hard place that night. I waited to talk to him after the service was over. Justin gave me his phone number — "

A few oohs and aahs from the younger ones interrupted Stephen's story.

"No, it wasn't anything like that. He just understands." The young man's eyes softened, and he slowly put his hands in his pockets.

I grabbed the plate of cookies and started walking toward the living room to my familiar seat, a brown chair with an ottoman. As we all got settled, I looked at Stephen and asked him to tell us more about that night when he was in a hard place.

After the students left, I got out my laptop and looked up the Gay Christian Network, the organization that Justin formed, and started reading. Who was he? I wanted to know. I cared about my students. I needed to better understand who they were listening to and what new ideas they found compelling.

The first time I was encouraged to read anything that I might disagree with was in my freshman New Testament class at ACU. Dr. Brecheen assigned John Stott's *Basic Christianity* and instructed us to put an exclamation mark beside the statements we agreed with, an *x* beside the things we disagreed with, and a question mark beside anything we questioned. Prior to that time, my tribe had always discouraged reading anything written by someone outside of the Church of Christ. We believed ideas expressed by such people were suspect and prone to leading us down the "slippery slope" of heresy. Long before I really understood what heresy meant, I knew what happened to those who went against something our tribe believed. I witnessed it happen to the worship leader who wrote one of my favorite devotional songs.

When I was in high school, our youth group had devotionals every Sunday night after our regular worship service. We would go to someone's home and have sandwiches or hamburgers and chips, with homemade cookies or brownies for dessert. Then we'd sit in a circle in the living room and sing to our hearts' content. Not the traditional hymns we sang during worship but the newer "devo" songs that became popular among youth groups in the 1970s. One of the most popular, and one of my favorites because it was upbeat, was "Blue Skies and Rainbows." I loved that song. We all did. We were still singing it at Tuesday night devos on the Administration Building steps when I was in college at ACU. By then it had become an old standard, a classic. I'll never forget meeting the guy who wrote it. He was one of our tribe.

In the summer of 1976, our youth group boarded our church's brand-new red-and-white air-conditioned school bus with "Tenth and Broad Church of Christ Wichita Falls, Texas" proudly painted on the side and traveled all the way to Winston-Salem, North Carolina. We and hundreds of other teenagers from around the country gathered for a national Christian youth conference. Every day we paired up and knocked on doors, inviting people to a gospel meeting in the evenings to hear Landon Saunders speak in the civic center. Every night – before Landon told us stories about Jesus that inspire me to this day – we sang familiar old hymns at the top of our lungs. We also sang new songs from youth group devos and church camp. In fact, the man who led our a cappella singing that week was the same man who wrote "Blue Skies and Rainbows."

Gary Mabry was a fantastic worship leader, although we would've called him a song leader at the time. I didn't know anything about him then except that he wrote that song. And that was enough for me. After a week of singing with him every night, I loved this guy even more. He was the best song leader I'd ever experienced, bringing such exuberance and energy to our praise time. That week was a pivotal point in solidifying my faith. While I didn't see Mabry again until much later in my life, I never forgot him.

A few years later – I'm not sure when, exactly – I started

hearing people say Gary Mabry had "gone off the deep end" and "left the church." He was "no longer one of us." I was sad to hear that, thinking, "He wrote 'Blue Skies and Rainbows,' and you're telling me he doesn't believe in God anymore?" I wouldn't find out until years later that he had merely started going to another church in a different denomination. But the way people talked about him made me think he had left his faith entirely. It instilled in me a real fear of being rejected, cast out, just for coming to see things differently. If I think differently, I can't be one of the tribe. If I didn't live strictly by the guidelines of the church, which were taken from our interpretation of Scripture, I would not be welcome. I would no longer belong.

I remember shuddering, my stomach turning over, as I imagined being cast out by this church family that meant everything to me. I never wanted to be in that spot. I made a promise to myself right then and there to never do anything that would bring about that kind of rejection.

But, in college, Dr. Brecheen's simple exercise opened the door for me to thoughtfully consider different points of view. In his class it was okay to evaluate John Stott's *Basic Christianity* and say what we agreed or disagreed with. Shortly thereafter, a class on argumentation and debate, required for my major, really brought home the importance of studying both sides of an issue. In competitive debate, we were required to argue both the affirmative and negative sides of a topic, supporting the resolution in one round of debate and refuting it in another. So, instead of choosing one side – a side that I might personally favor – and staying with that position, I also had to tear down the resolution, personal feelings aside. This was a challenge sometimes, but I eventually came to enjoy it. I liked learning and engaging critical thinking skills. I was able to assert not just what I believed but *why* I believed it.

The whole premise of presenting polar opposite perspectives of an issue is derived from Aristotle and his teaching on the search for truth. To Aristotle, finding Truth (with a capital *T*) is the highest ideal in society, and discovering it requires not only the presentation of facts from both ends of the spectrum of thought on an issue but also advocacy for each position. This is the foundation for our justice system today. It is adversarial in the sense that two polar opposite ideals or truths are pitted against each other, with an advocate for each position wholeheartedly presenting its case. By pitting these two "versions" of the truth against each other, Aristotle believed, a just society had the best opportunity to arrive at the Truth.

Truth has always been important to me. I was taught all my life that Truth is what my church was founded upon, and that our heritage is all about Alexander Campbell taking us back to the roots of Scripture to discern the truths about the early church. So, as I learned to evaluate different points of view in Dr. Brecheen's class or practiced debate in the argumentation course, I was grateful to be developing skills to help discern truth. Nothing mattered more than knowing the truth about what God wanted for my life.

"You don't really still believe that it's wrong to be in a same-sex relationship, do you, Sally?"

My friend's question caught me off guard. After all, I wasn't expecting a Bible professor, an Old Testament scholar to boot, to ask a question like that.

"Well, yeah, I do," I answered, taking a sip of my Dr. Pepper.

"Oh," he said, sounding a bit surprised. Allen heard our number called and walked up to the counter to pick up our sandwiches. When he got back to the table, we both started to talk at the same time.

"No, you go ahead," Allen insisted.

"I've read a few things, but I haven't come across anything that I find persuasive," I told him, putting my turkey sandwich back in the basket. "Nothing that I've read deals with Scripture in a way that makes sense and resonates with me. For me to be convinced that Scripture can say something different than what we've always believed, I'll need to read an author who deals with Scripture honestly and authentically."

"What have you read?" he asked.

"Not a lot that's affirming," I admitted. "Honestly, I've been hesitant to read anything that didn't go along with what I already believe. It scares me to think of what might happen if what I read made sense, you know?"

Here I was at ACU coaching debate after graduating from law school and having worked as an attorney. I had long come to understand the importance of evaluating both sides of an issue. I was immersed in an academic world that critically examined different perspectives. Yet Allen's question exposed the reality that I hadn't seriously studied affirming theology on same-sex relationships. When it came to examining what I believed about my sexuality, I remained fearful of discovering anything besides what I had always been taught, and always believed.

Up to this point, it had been fairly easy to avoid theological discussions about sexuality, because nobody from within my Church of Christ tribe had written or spoken about it. We didn't pay attention to faith-based material that was written by authors outside our walls. I didn't even know about any ministry efforts geared toward those of us attracted to our own sex because they existed outside of the Church of Christ. Those ministries were in existence in the 1970s and '80s, but I knew nothing about them. It would be the late 1990s before I heard about them.

I didn't have an iPhone as I do now, to search right there in the palm of my hand for information. By the time I had Internet access at home, I was in law school, and the only two sites I spent time on were WestLaw and LexisNexis, looking up cases. Amazon didn't exist back then, so I couldn't search for books on being gay. I would have had to go out in public – to a library or a bookstore – to retrieve material that might help me better understand myself. That was too risky. Someone I knew might see me, and then what? My shame and paranoia led me to believe such investigation would put an automatic target on my back.

But it wasn't just lack of access to information that kept me from exploring different points of view. I was afraid of anything I perceived might lead me astray. In fact, during law school I quit a job when I realized my boss was gay. During my second year of law school, I had started clerking for the attorney for students at Texas Tech University. She handled students' legal issues, as long as they didn't pose a conflict of interest with the university.

Landlord-tenant and contractual issues with businesses were the main things we dealt with in our office. I made phone calls and verified facts, talked to students, and looked up case law. It was an easy job that didn't pay much, but it gave me a lot of free time to study, and when the attorney wasn't busy, she talked to me about what I was studying, and that was always helpful.

When I first went to interview, I didn't know the attorney was gay. It was only after I had been there a while that I noticed her mention her partner, who was obviously another woman. One weekend they traveled to an Anne Murray concert in Las Vegas. For days before she left and after she got back, I could hear her own personal rendition of Murray's hits coming from her office. "Even though we ain't got money, I'm so in love with you, honey." She was always professional and kind. I liked the job. It made me feel at home, being in a nostalgic building, with a big office window overlooking a college campus full of students walking the grounds. I could ask her questions and feel like I had my own personal tutor on legal concepts that were confusing to me.

But when I eventually realized she was not only gay but in a relationship with another woman, that scared me. All my life I had heard the myths about the predatory nature of gay people "turning people that way." Nothing about this woman even remotely resembled that. She never did anything the least bit inappropriate with me. Yet I quit that job at the end of the semester, because of fear. I was afraid of working for a woman who was gay.

Looking back, I'm startled as to how fervently I believed in exploring every resource possible about an opposing view in a debate case or in a case going to trial, and yet I was terrified of anyone who might have a different view from mine on sexuality. That's where I was at the time, though. That's what made my conversation with Allen so important. It made me realize how much I was still living in fear. Even years later. But if I was seeking truth, what did I have to be afraid of? The whole point of looking at all the evidence and weighing each position on an issue was the very pursuit of truth. It wasn't long after my chat with Allen that the ACU student group meeting in my home prodded me to seriously investigate affirming theology.

To be credible in any conversation about faith and sexuality, especially among young people, I needed to understand what was being presented by the growing number of affirming voices. The students who had spent so much time around my dining room table, on my red couch, playing with my dog, Chester, were like my own children. They were devout and faithful Christ followers, some of whom planned to go into full-time ministry. The very least I could do was investigate the resources they were finding meaningful, even if—*especially if*—they were from outside our tribe. I needed to read with them, for them. And I needed to read for me.

So, I began reading everything I could find, on both sides.

I began keeping tabs on Justin Lee, the gay Christian man my students told me about. When his book *Torn* came out, I bought it. It was powerful, more memoir than hermeneutical discussion of Scripture. I remember thinking how much I resonated with Justin's story – his life, his family, his love for God, his sincere search for answers. He had a heart for reaching out to others, not just to those who viewed same-sex relationships as God honoring like he did. He made space for people who felt called to celibacy. Like me. Justin was concerned about fostering belonging based on our faith rather than our sexuality. I still was not fully convinced that a same-sex relationship was acceptable to God, but there was no doubt in my mind that Justin Lee was sincere in his devotion to God.

Later on, students told me about a video that had gone viral on YouTube of a young man preaching an hour-long sermon about how same-sex relationships could be pleasing to God. Matthew Vines aptly used Scripture to sanction same-sex relationships in a way I hadn't heard before. I recall noticing technical loopholes that kept me from being fully persuaded, but I also recall being moved by this young man's sincere love of the Bible and his desire to seek answers from Scripture. Neither Justin nor Matthew fits the stereotypes I often heard of gay people rejecting God.

When Justin's and Matthew's books came out, in 2012 and 2014, respectively, I read them primarily because many students I knew were reading them, and I wanted to be able to talk about the books with them. But my students' questions encouraged me to begin my own deeper study. So, I ordered a stack of books on Amazon and waited for their arrival. Maybe if I compared them with traditionalist Robert Gagnon's book, which had come out nearly two decades earlier, things would become clearer to me. Maybe if I could "flow" the arguments (an old debate term for the process of recording what is said by both sides and directly tying refutation to the original argument), I could actually see who "wins" the debate.

As I gathered and read a variety of Christian books that affirm same-sex relationships, it was quickly apparent that it was going to take time – an extraordinary amount of time – to sift through all the material. Often the scholarly books were dense and unfamiliar. Most were not compiled in the clear and concise form of legal writing that I had become accustomed to. In other words, I had a hard time getting through them. Even the books I finished had a dismissive tone toward the Bible or didn't address Scripture precisely enough to support an affirming view of same-sex relationships. For this good little Church of Christ girl, that was a deal breaker.

But eventually a book caught my attention. I'm a night owl, and I like to read in bed. The day I received James Brownson's book *Bible, Gender, and Sexuality* in the mail, I took it to bed with me, along with a cup of hot tea, and proceeded to read. I was quickly drawn to Brownson's obvious high regard for Scripture. I liked that he was never dismissive of the text. Instead, Brownson took every opportunity to emphasize Scripture's meaning and application for our lives today. By the end of the first chapter, it was clear to me that this book was different from many other affirming arguments I had read. I put it away and tried to sleep, but couldn't.

Every night for the next couple of weeks, I read a chapter before I went to sleep, with a glass of milk or a cup of tea and my dog, Chester, asleep in his bed on the floor beside mine. Brownson's writing style was clear and concise and made sense to me, making it possible for me to digest all of it with greater understanding. It was by far the most thorough review of the passages of Scripture that speak to sexuality that I'd read. I had been listening to preaching in my world that emphasized a holistic approach to studying the Bible for quite some time, so by the time I read Brownson, his call to read Scripture as a whole resonated with me. Instead of finding reasons to move away from Scripture to discover new meaning, this guy was continuously pointing back to Scripture and insisting on its relevance for our lives. Most of all, Brownson was willing to acknowledge when he didn't know something for certain. That meant the world to me.

Brownson's was only one of several books that made me realize the other side of the debate could offer a thoughtful, scripturally based affirming argument. I began to realize that not all those making the case for same-sex relationships were dismissive of the Bible or had liberal theology. I also found books not specifically about the same-sex debate that helped me to better read Scripture. Some of these authors were members of my tribe, the Church of Christ, and some belonged to other denominations – books like Richard Beck's *Unclean* and Mark Noll's *Civil War as a Theological Crisis*.

In the end, it wasn't just one book or sermon that changed my mind. A lifetime of experiences, conversations, classes, and exposure to people in different circumstances than my own helped me to read Scripture with fresh eyes. I came to understand the difference between the spirit of the law and the letter of the law. I also realized there is more to interpreting the Bible than proof texting – it involves awareness of historical context and translations. I came to recognize that Scripture is to be viewed as a whole – a story of God's love for and redemption of his creation. Rather than looking at Scripture as a rule book, picking verses out here and there, completely out of context, and trying to piece together an outline for my life, I can use Scripture better when taking its broader purpose to heart.

Yet, even as I was making these discoveries, I was fearful of becoming affirming. What would that do to CenterPeace, the ministry I had poured my heart into? What would happen to me and my place in the Church of Christ? Would my people say, as they did about Gary Mabry, that I had "gone off the deep end," that I didn't belong anymore? It would have been easier to put everything down and continue believing just as I did. But I couldn't do that. If I was going to be faithful to my students, to the families who trusted me over the years, and to myself, I couldn't just stick my head in the sand. No matter how scary the outcome might be, I knew I couldn't keep quiet much longer.

Part 3

Embracing Covenant

Two are better than one,
because they have a good return for their labor:
If either of them falls down,
one can help the other up.
But pity anyone who falls
and has no one to help them up.
Also, if two lie down together, they will keep warm.
But how can one keep warm alone?

(Eccles. 4:9–11)

9

What Healing Looks Like for Me

It was a different time, back in 1996, when I walked into David's counseling office in Dallas that first time, a bundle of nerves, full of shame and feeling sheer terror at the thought of anyone discovering that I was attracted to women. People still didn't talk much about such things. My heart pounded out of my chest when I opened the door to the counseling office, praying to God I wouldn't see anyone I knew. Of course, as luck would have it, I saw three people I knew – people I hadn't seen in ages – and I was aghast. Two of them were on staff at the office and the other was sitting in the waiting area. It felt as if I had "LESBIAN" tattooed across my forehead.

Just going to therapy alone was uncommon and suspect in my world at that time. Back then, not being able to conquer your feelings with God's help through prayer was indicative of weak faith, or a sign of serious mental illness. So, I didn't want anyone to know I was going to counseling, and I certainly didn't want them to know why. I hoped the counselor, David, would tell me what to do to make this attraction to women go away, and help cultivate a stronger attraction to men. I would have done almost anything asked of me to make that happen.

I had dated boys in high school and in college that I cared about deeply. But I never felt the same about them as I felt for girls. When I first had a crush on a girl in high school, I knew the feeling was totally different from anything I had felt for a boy. The connection I had with guys was more emotional than sexual. But because of the time it was, and because no one dared mention someone being attracted to their own gender, I didn't understand my feelings. I had no idea what was happening. But now I hoped therapy would clear everything up.

At the time I sought counseling, the ex-gay movement was beginning to gain prominence. Founded in the early 1970s, the movement asserted that a combination of prayer and elements of reparative therapy could bring healing for those seeking freedom from same-sex attraction. Reparative therapy says a person experiences same-sex attraction because of perceived gender inferiority, sometimes from not relating to same-sex peers growing up or from a disconnect with the same-sex parent. This may be "repaired" by forming healthy relationships with people of the same sex and healing parent-child wounds. Typically, the therapy encourages men to embrace their masculinity and women their femininity, as defined by stereotypical gender norms.

When I walked into David's office, I had never heard of reparative therapy. I didn't know about Exodus International, the largest umbrella organization for the ex-gay movement, or any of its subsidiary ministries all over the country. Word hadn't spread to my insular world, largely because the Church of Christ didn't look outside of our tribe, to the larger Christian domain, for resources or help on problematic issues. Exodus had already been around for twenty years by the time I learned of its existence. But what I didn't realize was how much the ex-gay movement was already in the air so many of us were breathing, and would inadvertently affect my counseling experience.

My counselor, David, never used the phrase "reparative" or "conversion" therapy with me, but many of our conversations over the years included how I felt about my femininity and feelings of inadequacy as a female. Early on this was always in conjunction with discussion of my troubled relationship with my father, and the impact his intermittent bouts of rage had had on me, particularly in my childhood. Later on, he recommended, and I read, books rooted in ex-gay philosophy, such as *Portraits of Freedom*, *Coming Out of Homosexuality*, and *The Broken Image*. The last one was by Leanne Payne, a straight, single mother turned pastoral care provider, who was a beloved figure in the ex-gay movement. People flocked to her healing prayer ministry.

At that time in my life, I truly believed that if I could discover why I was attracted to women – what had *caused* my attraction to women – and repair whatever the cause, that attraction would go away. I didn't want to have these feelings, I just had them. I hadn't asked for them. And I believed I had to make them go away. Like so many others on this same path, I would follow whatever directive I needed to, to make this part of myself disappear. In therapy, I came to believe my perception of femininity and my broken relationship with my dad were the source of my problem. I thought if I could build a relationship with Daddy and address feelings of gender inadequacy, my "natural" feelings of attraction to the opposite sex would increase.

When I look back at my first memoir, *Loves God, Likes Girls*, I see now how much I interpreted my life experiences through the lens of reparative therapy. It's not that the things I wrote about in my first book weren't true or didn't happen; it's that my interpretation of those things has changed. Even after I had experienced healing in my relationship with Daddy and had dealt with the resulting lies I believed about men and myself as a woman, I did not experience a change in sexual orientation. I was healed. Just not in the way I expected.

I thought my attraction to women was because of my lack of a safe, loving, and consistent relationship with my dad. I believed this skewed my view of men, making me fearful, and incapable of experiencing romantic or physical attraction to a man. So, I worked on my relationship with my father, and to his credit, Daddy worked on our relationship, too. I will never forget the things we did to recapture a childhood that had been interrupted again and again by his rage and silence. We intentionally did things to repair those interruptions and replace the lies I had bought into about his love for me, and about men in general, with truth. Truth that my dad loved me and always had, and that men could be safe and loving and nurturing.

When Daddy and I first sat with David in those counseling sessions to work on our relationship, I remember being so hurt and angry that my father had never called me on the phone. In college I sat in amazement at my roommate talking to her dad, who had called her, and in the middle of the day. Their conversations were easy, not forced, as natural as my conversations with my mom had always been on the phone. I shared this pain during counseling, and after that, Daddy started calling me.

It was hard at first, both of us uncomfortable, not knowing what to talk about. But then I asked Daddy if he would read the Harry Potter books with me, a chapter a night, and then we could talk about them on the phone. To my amazement, he didn't think it silly, so I bought us each a book and we began to read. And we learned to talk on the phone. For the first time in my life, I began to learn how to really share my thoughts, and eventually my feelings, with my daddy. I was in my late thirties.

Fast-forward twenty years, and hardly a day passes that I don't talk to my dad. He's ninety, and in the seven years since my mother's death, we've talked as never before. A couple of years ago we spent a week in Hawaii and had a grand time. As a navy veteran, he loved seeing the Pearl Harbor memorial and showing me around the USS *Missouri*, a ship my dad had gone aboard during his term of service in the Korean War. If someone had told me when I was thirty years old that someday I would take a trip with my dad, just the two of us, and feel completely at ease, completely content, I would've told them they were crazy. But we did.

Yet for all of the healing in my relationship with Daddy, I'm still gay.

When my mom and I went shopping in my childhood, we always went to Parker Square. It was closer than downtown, and McClurkans' department store was there. We usually parked right outside the boys' department, because that was the closest spot to the post office and the hair salon. Mama would stop off first to mail letters, and then we'd make our way through the department store. On one of our excursions when I was about eight or nine years old, something caught my eye in the boys' section on the way in, and I asked my mom if we could look. It was the coolest pair of shorts I'd ever seen. First, they seemed longer, like the Bermuda shorts my dad wore in the summer, and they were covered in Campbell's tomato soup cans. The name Andy Warhol meant nothing to me at the time, and it would be much later before I realized the shorts were made from a fabric print of his famous painting. All I knew at the time was that I had never seen anything like them, and, oh, I wanted those shorts.

Much to my mom's credit, she let me try them on. They fit and I was ecstatic. I remember her asking me if I was really going to wear them. "They're kinda loud. Are you sure you'll wear them?" she asked. I told her I loved these shorts, and we bought them. For the rest of the summer they were like my uniform. At the time, it didn't register with me that these shorts were in the boys' department. I just saw them, liked that they were different, and therefore wanted to wear them. For as long as I can remember, I've preferred my own sense of style, somewhere in the middle of wearing enough to "fit in" and being unique.

Mama never made a big deal about what I wore. When it came to a special occasion like a wedding, I knew I was expected to wear a dress, and that was okay. Because even the dresses she let me pick out weren't frilly or overly "girly" in the least. She always said my taste made sense to her because she had always preferred styles that were tailored. When I traipsed into the hallway at the age of eight, having ransacked my father's closet, dressed in one of his blazers with a shirt and tie and his shoes, instead of seeming disturbed that I wasn't dressing up in her clothes, she proudly took my picture. I was different, she said, and that was okay.

Mama even let me wear overalls to church. Not the brand-new store-bought ones that were in style for girls in the late 1970s, but my grandfather's old pair from the 1930s, tattered and worn, with holes in the leg and the seat that she had patched. I remember my senior English teacher brushing up against me once at my desk when I was wearing them, along with a pair of tennis shoes with huge holes, to say quietly, "Sally, I know your parents make more money than that." But my mom let me wear them. Along with a newsboy cap and anything else I wanted, as long as it was modest. All Mama cared about was who I was on the inside, my character, and putting God first in my life.

Yet despite Mama's affirmation of me, I felt inadequate growing up and into young adulthood. Much of that came from my childhood perception of what it meant to be feminine, or what it looked like to be a woman. As we know, children are tremendous observers of their surroundings but not so good at interpreting those surroundings. I learned that women should be and do certain things. I learned this by watching the women around me and the girls at school and the narratives I saw on TV.

My picture of what was "necessary" was shaped by my era — my social context, with all the cultural expectations of gender roles from the 1960s and 1970s. My era was full of the societal remnants of *Father Knows Best* and *Leave It to Beaver*, while transitioning into *Laugh-In*; *Love, American Style*; and *The Mary Tyler*

Moore Show. My culture was full of personal role models who looked a lot more like June Cleaver than Mary Richards. So, I strived to be something of a combination of the two. I learned how to start from the outside of the silverware and work my way in when seated at a fancy dinner table. I learned I could spend a fortune cutting my hair if I wanted to. Truthfully, I like a lot of things that my world would describe as feminine preferences, things like shopping and decorating and having lunch with friends at a cozy, quaint little tea room.

The ideology of reparative therapy, which had subtly infused the counseling I was receiving, led me to believe that everyone fits into a mold of either masculine or feminine, and it's the rejection of my gender that contributes to same-sex attraction. So, of course, I tried to rid myself of the things that culture deems more masculine, so I could return to my "natural" roots of "femininity," and thus my attraction to women would disappear. Part of my healing has indeed involved proving to the little girl in me that I can achieve those stereotypical norms just as well as the next woman. But a bigger part of healing for me has been the realization that it's not the ability to do things that the culture labels "feminine" that makes me a woman. Being a woman is not limited to certain tasks or traits.

Often, in this same culture, that would also mean the loss of my assertiveness, my leadership skills, my public speaking ability, my sense of humor, and other qualities that the world in which I grew up has attributed to men. I am all these things, but I am also a woman, and proud of that fact. The truth is, I am a woman like my mother and my grandmother and my aunt, and all the other women whose uniqueness made them stand out a little bit from their peers. Coming back to my mother's wisdom of allowing me to be me, to be different, to love my uniqueness, and to esteem the gifts God has given me is perhaps the greatest healing of all.

Twenty years ago, I had no idea what healing would look like for me. I anticipated it would involve diminishing same-sex attractions and being able to fall in love with a man. At the very least, I thought healing might enable me to do what Christian songwriter Dennis Jernigan did: find just *one* person of the opposite sex that I was attracted to enough to marry. But that is not what happened. Later I learned that most people don't experience a change in sexual orientation. I even contemplated whether a mixed-orientation marriage might work, where one spouse is attracted to their own gender and the other spouse is heterosexual. But even though some couples have been able to make it work, many of those marriages end tragically in divorce, leaving children in the wake. I knew I wouldn't be able to pull off a mixed-orientation marriage.

I've learned more about sexual orientation over the last several years, and the depth of what it means for a person to be gay. Our sexual orientation determines far more about us than our sexual behavior. It is a fundamental aspect of how we are drawn to and relate to others. I've learned there can be more biological elements involved than I understand or am qualified to discuss. My attraction to the same sex can't be explained away simply as the result of childhood wounds and feelings of gender inferiority. It makes sense, then, that even as I healed in the ways that reparative therapy recommended, I am still gay.

Instead of making me straight, counseling helped me become more trusting and open with others. Because of the fear of rejection I had felt with my dad, and my rejection of myself as unique, I was afraid to be vulnerable with people. I had many friends, but I was unwilling to go deep with them. I could be their sounding board, their listening ear, but I dared not share my own deepest feelings and thoughts. The irony of my healing is that the more I was able to open myself up and become vulnerable with friends, the more I longed for, and became capable of, real intimacy. Not only the intimacy I experienced with the dearest of friends. I longed for more, in a way that I had never felt before. Instead of being rid of the desire to be in an exclusively intimate relationship with another woman, I began to yearn for that all the more.

10

"It's Not Good for Man to Be Alone"

I'll never forget the conversation I had with fourteen-year-old Jordan. The day before our conversation we had met at his church, where I'd been invited to do a weekend CenterPeace seminar to help church leaders and congregants better understand what it means to be LGBTQ, and how they might respond more lovingly to the LGBTQ community. Jordan had recently come out to his family, and they all attended. Afterward, his parents approached me and asked if I would spend some time with their son. I said I would be glad to. So, they dropped him off with me at a frozen yogurt shop, and we spent a good part of the afternoon talking.

Jordan was the kind of kid that I would've loved having in my class back when I taught high school speech and debate. He could carry on a conversation, and a smile came easily for him. We chatted about what life was like for him growing up in a southern rural culture that held certain expectations of masculinity, when his inclinations were quite the opposite. We also talked about school, what he might like to do with his life someday, and if and where he'd like to go to college.

"Well, I'd like to go to college," he started, "but I don't think I want to go to a Christian school."

"Why is that?" I asked.

"It's pretty hard for somebody who's gay to go to a Christian school. You can't talk about being gay."

"Well, you might be surprised. That's changing in some places," I answered, trying not to close out all the possibilities.

Knowing in my head that his concerns were valid but hoping in my heart that it might be different by the time he got to college, I tried to paint a more optimistic picture of Christian higher education for him.

"I know plenty of people in Christian universities who are LGBTQ. I know schools that have organizations on campus. And I have professor friends at Christian universities who are strong advocates for LGBTQ students. If you wanted to go for the Christian aspect – to be in an atmosphere that would help strengthen your faith – well, don't let that scare you off."

Jordan glanced down at his cup of yogurt, swirling his spoon around in it. He looked vulnerable. My heart went out to this kid who had to sit with an old lady in the yogurt shop, a perfectly rank stranger, because he told his parents he's gay.

I finished my chocolate yogurt while his bowl was still half full, melting away as he continued to dabble in it. Still looking down, he started to speak hesitantly.

"Can I ask you something?" he said quietly.

A seriousness came over him, and I said he could ask me anything.

He looked up at me with apprehension in his eyes.

"Does this mean I have to spend the rest of my life by myself?"

I caught my breath, and my heart sank.

Jordan wasn't just asking about sex; he was asking about living a life of aloneness. A life that excluded him from sharing the day-to-day with someone who knows him intimately. Someone to create a home and grow old with him. Life seems long at the age of fourteen. Turning fifteen takes an eternity, let alone getting to twenty-five or thirty-five or – God forbid – the ancient age of fifty. Jordan was contemplating the future stretched out in front of him, wondering whether he would have a companion to share that road with him.

I felt the answer to his question in the pit of my stomach. I was living the answer. I knew full well the pain that accompanies a life lived alone. His question hit me at a time when I was just beginning to wake up to how lonely I really was. How desperately alone I had been all my life. As I contemplated how to respond, it was as though my life thus far flashed before me, and I saw the aching loneliness I had felt as a child, as a teenager, as a young adult, and now, as a middle-aged woman, single and still living alone. I was always surrounded by people with a host of friends and embraced by a church family. But still alone.

Suddenly it dawned on me that my life had answered his question precisely in the way my generation had been conditioned to live it out. According to prior generations in my world, the only answer to Jordan's question was "Yes, you're going to have to live the rest of your life by yourself if you want to have a place with your church family, to not be questioned, to not be judged, to not be confronted and potentially cast out of the church you grew up in. You're going to have to be all by yourself."

When I was twenty-two years old, I moved into an apartment by myself for the first time. I was in graduate school, working as a teaching assistant, and had friends who had stayed in town after graduation to work. I was heavily involved at church, and participated in an active singles ministry. I also volunteered to help teach the eighth-grade girls' Bible class on Wednesday nights. But despite all the activity, I was lonely in that apartment. After Sunday service I stayed and talked to people, just as I had with my family growing up, usually until they started turning the lights out on us. But afterward, when I would get in my car to drive home, those same pangs of loneliness would hit. I got to where I couldn't stand Sunday afternoons. I couldn't stand going home alone, when all my memories were of being part of a family – a family that went to Luby's or Piccadilly Cafeteria every Sunday after church.

Over the years, I've known how to keep up a good front, but on the inside, I felt so alone. So, I threw myself into my work, coaching high school speech and debate, and directing theater, going to law school, teaching college-level communication classes, and investing every part of myself into my students. I also filled my desire for another's presence in the house with the noise of the TV. The sound of people's voices was comforting. Lots of times I was doing something else, even reading, but the TV was still on, so that I wouldn't feel quite so alone. I woke up to *The Today Show* and went to sleep to the sound of David Letterman's voice. I even got a dog named Chester, the world's greatest.

It wasn't that I didn't have friends. I did. I had a wealth of social and professional connections. All my life I've made friends easily. I might not have always felt comfortable in making myself vulnerable, but I've always had friends. Friends I met for lunch. Friends I went to movies with. Friends whose homes I was familiar with from eating dinners there and just hanging out. Friends I called when I was visiting out of town and needed a place to stay. Friends I loved dearly. I've been involved in women's Bible classes, attended women's retreats, developed friendships at work and at church. I've had friends my age, younger, and older. Friends with whom I've shared the darkest places of my heart. Friends with whom I've wept tears of sorrow and joy, and laughed till both of my sides hurt.

But what I've ached for is more than friendship. I want my life to be sacredly intertwined with another for life. To form a family unit. Biblical scholar James Brownson notes that when Adam recognizes Eve as "bone of my bones and flesh of my flesh" (Gen. 2:23), he is using the language of kinship. I sincerely thought, like many others, that having a close circle of friends would fill this longing for kinship. That having a close-knit community who shared life together, perhaps even living nearby each other in the same apartment complex or neighborhood, would meet that need. But surprisingly enough, it has been during times that I've felt most connected and content in my community that I have fallen deeply in love with a woman. I truly had everything, but something was still missing.

The truth is, a friendship, even a best friendship, is a different kind of relationship than marriage. Who among the married would claim there is no difference between a spouse and a best pal? They are different, and not just because of a sexual relationship. That difference is what I was missing and yearning for. I longed to build a whole life with someone, to make a home. Someone to exchange glances and a smile with from across a crowded room of people at a party, knowing I came with her and I would leave with her. I longed for someone to sit in the living room with in the evenings and read silently together. All the little things that we cherish that bring comfort and solace in a marriage. Someone to come home to at the end of the day.

I walked into the room where the elders were already seated around long tables. I had been invited by the leadership to give a workshop on ministry to LGBTQ people. This church had selected twenty men to serve as shepherds, and they were all present. They varied in age, with a few younger than I, but most were somewhat older.

I shared my story and discussed the importance of open, honest dialogue about faith and sexuality in our churches. Talking about LGBTQ concerns is crucial for the sake of our young people, I stressed. They are leaving the church over this. We spent time talking about our fears around the topic of same-sex sexuality and some of the misperceptions we've had that keep LGBTQ people at arm's length in our faith communities.

When I finished the presentation, I opened up the floor

for questions. One elder expressed confusion about why some people consider the expectation of celibacy for gay people a problem. "Why is expecting people who experience same-sex attraction to be celibate unfair?" he asked. "It's no different than being heterosexual and single, is it?"

A few other elders began speaking up, insisting that it wasn't the same. "Well, it's different because they have to keep how they feel a secret," one elder commented.

The elders continued to engage the question. Everyone listened politely, sincerely trying to understand where each person was coming from.

The one who initiated the question continued. "You know, I have family members who are single, who have never been married in their lives, and I don't feel sorry for them. Maybe they didn't choose to be married or didn't have the opportunity, but they're not hurting because of that. Why is it so different to ask a gay person to be celibate?"

I wanted to ask if he had actually had those conversations with the single members of his family, inquiring about their happiness in being single, or if he was perhaps making an assumption. I wanted to tell him that no one had ever asked me if I was okay being single. Or if I ever got lonely or wished I was married and had a family. Maybe that's because I gave the impression of being perfectly fine with my singleness and being independent, even when that's not how I've always felt.

I waited to see if the elders had any further comments, then offered a response. "It's different because for a heterosexual person who's single, there's always the chance that they will meet someone, fall in love, and then have the option to marry. That's always a possibility, with nothing hindering them except finding someone. But for an LGBTQ person who is a Christian and believes in a traditional sexual ethic, there's no hope," I said. "There's no hope in ever being able to have the companionship that God designed us to need. For LGBTQ people living under a traditional Christian sexual ethic, that possibility doesn't exist. We know this early on, when we are still young, in our teens and twenties, that if we live under the traditional guidelines of the church that confine marriage to a man and a woman, we will never be able to have that type of relationship."

There was silence in the room.

"You know, Sally, being single is a whole lot easier to talk about when you're married," one of the older elders interjected. A smile came across his face, and I smiled back. Several others grinned and nodded their heads.

"I think you're right, Roy," I answered. "Maybe some people can live a single life more easily – maybe they're just fine with it. But I know lots of people who are desperately lonely as single persons."

More heads nodded. I could tell this was a room full of men who took their job of listening as shepherds seriously.

"When we call LGBTQ people to celibacy, we're not just saying, 'You can't have sex.' It goes so much deeper. We're telling someone, 'You're going to have to live your life alone.' If I went around and asked each one of you to tell me what you value most about your relationship with your spouse, would sex be the most important aspect of your marriage?"

I looked at each one of them in turn sitting around the table. Then my eyes reached the elder whose wife had passed away not too long ago. They had been married forty years. His eyes were teary. I paused, looking gently at him. "What you miss about Barbara is so much more than sex, isn't it, Sam?" I asked. "You miss sitting down to supper every night with someone. Deciding where you're going to eat after church on a Sunday afternoon. Sitting outside on the patio in the spring, looking over the yard and talking about what you want to plant in the flowerbeds. Planning vacations and what you're going to get the grandkids for Christmas. Just having someone in the room watching television in silence. Knowing there's someone beside you when you're sick. Being able to tell someone about your day. The person who knows all your stories and may roll their eyes when you tell them at the family gathering over the holidays."

Sam nodded, holding back tears.

I remember the first time I fell deeply in love with a woman who was capable of returning my affection. I had fallen in love a few times before, but it was with straight women friends who had no idea of my attraction. I knew there was never any chance of reciprocation. With Jill, suddenly possibility hung in the air. I felt all the things people feel when they meet someone they're deeply attracted to. Dry mouth, heart racing, palms sweating, tongue-tied – all of it. While this felt good, another part of me was scared senseless, scared because Jill was attracted to women as well. At the time I still believed God didn't want me to be in a relationship with a woman.

Jill and I had only recently crossed paths. I wanted to be

friends with her, but I wasn't sure what to do. I decided to talk it over with David, my counselor, hoping for clarity.

"I need to tell you about something," I told David.

"Okay, shoot," he replied.

"I don't know how this happened, but I've met this woman, and I can't stop thinking about her. I am so drawn to her, but it scares me," I explained.

"Well, what are you afraid of?" David asked.

"I'm afraid of having feelings for her," I said, "and where that might lead. I can't be friends with a woman I am strongly attracted to."

"Why can't you?" he continued, seemingly unconcerned.

"Well, what if she develops feelings for me? That would be really hard to navigate – both of us being attracted to each other but feeling like we weren't supposed to act on those feelings. How in the world would we do that?" I questioned, growing a little agitated but accustomed to his Socratic style of counseling by now.

"Just because you have feelings for her doesn't mean you have to act on them."

I thought a moment and knew that to be true. "Yeah, you're right," I said.

"You can have a close intimate friendship with someone you have feelings for," David told me, "without ever having sex with them. Developing a close, nonsexual connection will help both of you to meet your legitimate emotional needs in a healthy way." Even though he didn't mention reparative therapy outright, his advice mirrored it.

At the time I didn't know if that was true or not, but I put my full trust in David. After all, he had rescued my family. He had worked miracles in my relationship with my dad. Why wouldn't I trust him here, too? I trusted anything David said.

I felt a sense of relief when he didn't counsel me to discontinue the friendship. In fact, he strongly encouraged my friendship with Jill and even teasingly referred to her as my girlfriend. This gave me permission to grow closer to Jill, and soon we were talking every day. It felt wonderful to have someone in my life with whom I connected on every important level. I loved Jill's heart for God, her quick intellect, her love of children and old people. I loved how kind she could be and also how snarky. I loved the way she looked and the way she held me when we hugged. And yet I was determined never to act on the very real desire I felt for her. I wanted with all my heart to serve God, to be who I believed he calls me to be. And Jill felt the same.

For the first time in my life, I felt like I was connecting with a woman in a way that was truly reciprocal, and the mutuality felt wonderful. I had someone to care for and who cared for me. Someone who considered me in her plans and whom I considered in mine. We promised we would never walk away from each other. That we would always be there for each other in life. For a short while it seemed like David's advice would work. That we could just love each other deeply as friends. But the closeness only intensified our relationship. Our hugs grew longer.

One day, after we had taken a nap together on the couch, she called me while I was driving home and told me that she had feelings for me. My heart leapt into my throat, pounding. I was absolutely overjoyed to hear those words. I told her I felt the same. It was exhilarating to know that a woman I loved not only thought of me in that way but also took the initiative to express that before I did. Yet, as Jill demonstrated desire to go further physically, I resisted. I wanted to live by my convictions and I knew, ultimately, that she did too. It wasn't long, though, before my resolve faltered. When our love was finally expressed physically, it felt like the most natural thing in the world.

I kept waiting for the guilt I had always expected to feel to come, but it didn't. We had already expressed a commitment to be there for each other over a lifetime. It just felt wonderful to have taken this next step in the relationship. I was so tired of being alone. Despite years of effort, I hadn't been able to rid myself of the deep longing to be in a loving, committed relationship. I just wanted someone who was "my person" – the person I "tell all my stories to," as Dar Williams sings, the person to sit beside in church, whose hand I always want to hold. At the time, I believed Jill felt the same way, that she was committed for life too, for she said it, and in every way, she lived that out month after month. Until one day she didn't.

Looking back, I recognize aspects of the relationship that sabotaged it from the beginning. Foremost was the secrecy. Neither of us felt safe telling our families. Some friends knew, but very few. We hadn't gone through the normal dating or courtship rituals where couples take time to discover they're compatible. We couldn't do that openly. Jill also continued to have deep-seated misgivings about being in a same-sex relationship. So, after a time, not having people to walk alongside us and help us openly live in covenant relationship, and the strain of feeling as if we were living a double life, combined to make the relationship difficult, and she left. When she walked away, a devastating sense of loss and loneliness flooded me.

To lose that kind of love is the most excruciating pain I've ever felt. It's like the scene in the movie *Castaway*, where Tom Hanks's character is stranded on an island in the middle of the ocean. After years of not being rescued, he ventures off the island in a crudely constructed raft, and following days at sea with no food or water, baked from the scorching sun, he falls asleep. Upon waking, he discovers that the volleyball he painted a face on years before – "Wilson" – who became his only companion on the island, had slipped off the pedestal it was fastened to and was drifting farther and farther from the raft. At first, he jumps in the water in an attempt to save Wilson, calling desperately to it, as if a volleyball could hear him, but finally he gives up. Realizing that if he continues to go after Wilson he will drift farther from the raft, losing his only hope of survival, he swims back and sobs all alone on the raft.

I have never been able to watch that scene without being moved to tears. So often I have felt that same sense of loss, the gravity of not being able to have a relationship I so desired. I have often felt adrift in an ocean, trying to fill the God-given impulse to deeply know and be known by another person, while having to count the cost of either pursuing my "Wilson" or swimming back to the raft of family, friends, and church who would not otherwise accept me. Treading water, trying to discern what was right in those moments, was so exhausting. Only to be left alone again, on the raft, out in the middle of a grueling and never-ending sea of despair. I cry every time I see that scene in the movie because it depicts so accurately the conflict and tension that every LGBTQ person raised in a conservative Christian home faces when the only option we are told that pleases God is a life of aloneness.

The love I felt for Jill was real. It was the same love that exists in any heterosexual relationship, that brings any two people together. But the love we shared for each other was always tainted with the belief that the relationship we were in was not permissible. As much as I wanted to justify the relationship because of my sincere desire to commit to her for life, it was still wrong. Not because a committed relationship between two women is wrong. Not because we weren't technically married with legal documentation from the state. It was wrong because of the secrecy. It was wrong because we couldn't be open and fully embrace each other, both literally and figuratively, as partners for life. And because of that, we couldn't fully receive the support that every couple needs from family and friends to help us live in covenant as God desires for us.

Over the years I've had the opportunity to form friendships with people far more knowledgeable of Scripture than I am. People who have studied the Bible longer, and studied it more deeply, than I have. People who have preached more sermons than I have heard in my lifetime, and I've heard plenty. These are the people I have trusted and sought out to help answer my questions, to help resolve the tension I have felt between my faith and sexuality. One of my most faithful conversation partners is a former Bible professor.

"Sally, the one passage that I believe is controlling in the question of same-sex marriage is Genesis 1–3," Terry said. "The creation story of Adam and Eve sets the parameters for marriage right there – marriage is between a man and a woman."

We had barely finished lunch before Terry wandered back into the living room to continue our conversation. For the last two days we had been talking about all the passages of Scripture dealing with same-sex sexuality, but now we were approaching the topic of marriage from a much broader perspective, looking at the "totality" of Scripture, as Terry insisted. After his wife, Joan, finished clearing the table and putting our lunch dishes in the dishwasher, she joined our conversation.

"Okay," I agreed. "I'll give you that. Let's say that the first three chapters of Genesis do dictate what we need to know about marriage."

Terry stopped pacing around the room and came over to sit down on the end of the sectional sofa next to Joan, folding his arms and putting one finger over his lips, looking very professorial.

"If Genesis 1–3 tells us what to believe about gender and marriage, why do we not hold as rigorously to what God says about loneliness right in the same passage?" I asked sincerely. "In Genesis 2:18, God says it isn't good for man to be alone. That's the whole reason he made Eve, to be a companion for Adam, right? So that means God recognized that Adam needed someone besides the animals, right? And that not even God himself could meet Adam's need for companionship, doesn't it?"

"You're right, Sally," Terry said. "That's the way I understand the passage."

"But why doesn't the part about God saying 'It's not good for man to be alone' stand out as equally important?" I wanted to know. "You're favoring one part over the other."

Terry told me he believed the passage was specifically talking about the man and the woman being suitable companions for one another, and that this was the most important part.

"But *what if*," I continued, "the most important part is about not being alone? What if that's the lens that should dictate our interpretation of Genesis?"

It was quiet, and I saw Joan glance at her husband. Terry stared at me, and soon I could see the twinkle in his eyes, his hand still hiding the slight smile on his face.

"I don't know," Terry said.

We spent the rest of the afternoon talking about the human need for companionship.

11

Covenant

I looked at the map of Waco, searching for the right restaurant that was halfway between Dallas and Austin. I was nervous, worrying about what I was wearing and what my hair looked like. No, Sally, you have no idea whether this woman would even be interested in you. I tried to keep from getting too excited about meeting Karen for the first time. Just be cool, I thought. Don't be too interested. Just feel her out first, I told myself while driving down I-35. It was January 2019, and Karen had messaged me to say she was visiting family in Texas and wanted to know if we could meet halfway for dinner. A year earlier we had started following each other on Twitter as a result of our shared ministry work with the LGBTQ community. She kept popping up in my Twitter feed. The more I saw Karen's posts, the more I appreciated her spirit, her desire to see LGBTQ Christians spiritually formed, for all to experience the love of God.

Several months after we first made contact, in August 2018, Karen sent me a direct message on Twitter, asking me to consider being on the launch team for her new book coming out that fall, *Scripture, Ethics, and the Possibility of Same-Sex Relation-*

ships. Before consenting, I wanted to know more about the book and the posture she took. So, we scheduled time to talk over the phone. I paced my living room during that first conversation, partly because I was nervous and eager to find out if she was really who she appeared to be in her tweets. Because if she was, it might just be that we had a lot in common. I was also nervous because she was grilling me on my first memoir, trying to understand my beliefs and approach to ministry. But I liked that. She held my feet to the fire about things I had written. I had to defend certain things and explain other things, namely, that I wasn't part of the ex-gay movement. After that phone call, my curiosity about Karen grew. I began to learn more about her ministry work as an educator and spiritual care provider.

Now, here I was driving to meet her in person. I arrived first, a rarity for me, and got a table in the back of a room filled with ranchers and their families, along with people who most likely lived in town. The place I found for us to eat, George's, was a classic Texas diner with plate lunch specials, fried catfish, and chicken-fried steak. Since Karen lived on the East Coast, I thought she might enjoy some local flavor, seeing men in cowboy hats and boots, and smelling like grease when we walked out of the place. When she arrived, she looked just like her picture that was becoming my favorite on social media, showing off her shoulder-length dark straight hair, tall thin frame, studious glasses, and behind them, deep blue eyes. My heart raced when I saw her walk in, and as soon as I caught her eye, we grinned at each other.

"Hello!" she said exuberantly, taking her navy blue peacoat off and placing it in the chair beside her at our table.

She was wearing a nubby brown sweater with flecks of cream and burnt orange, and a pair of beige corduroy jeans. She sat down in the seat directly across from me, and I handed her a menu and reminded myself that maybe she just wanted this to be about collaborating in our ministry work. But I was okay with that. I focused on enjoying our conversation over dinner. For three hours we sat and talked about our lives, our experiences as LGBTQ Christians, our love of ministry, books, and writing. Our plates had long been cleared and the check paid by the time we finally decided to leave. We put our coats on and walked out of the diner and into the parking lot to find our cars. Before she walked away to her car parked across the street, she turned and hugged me, telling me how much she appreciated meeting for dinner, and thanked me for the conversation. Likewise, I replied, and watched her smile sweetly before she turned to walk to her car.

On the drive home I thought about all the things we talked about, all the interests we had in common, and how, most of all, we shared a mutual love for God. But she lived miles away, and I wasn't sure what level of interest she might have in even developing a friendship with me. Yet, hoping to keep a door open, I had asked her during dinner if she would serve as a spiritual director for our upcoming spiritual formation retreat for LGBTQ Christians. And she agreed to come. I was grateful I would have the chance to see her again in a few months.

In some ways, it was hard to imagine something could really happen, that Karen and I might ever start dating. For so much of my life, I was told it wasn't possible. I grew up hearing that anyone attracted to the same sex couldn't possibly be a Christ follower or capable of lifelong commitment. The picture painted for me of gay people was one of promiscuity, debauchery, lasciviousness, and licentiousness, long before I ever knew what those words actually meant. A gay couple couldn't possibly feel the same love as a heterosexual couple, so I was told. This made coming to understand myself difficult and confusing because I *did* want a committed, Christ-centered relationship. I wanted the sacred things my church tribe had taught me about Christian marriage. I never wanted anything else. I simply longed for it in a marriage to a woman and not a man.

At the time I met Karen, I wasn't actively looking for a relationship. Despite my desire for marriage, I've never sought out dating. In fact, up to that point in my life, I had only had one relationship with a woman. But every woman I have felt romantically drawn to, whether she knew of my affection or not, has had one thing in common with me. She loved God. She was devoutly Christian, and that was evident in her life. We shared a deep faith and commitment to our church communities. This is what I have first loved about anyone I have been drawn to. Always. I have never been attracted to someone who isn't first and foremost a Christ follower.

It was a warm May morning when my summer intern and I picked up Karen at the airport. Four months earlier, in that Waco restaurant, I had invited her to help serve at a Center-Peace Tapestry retreat. Now the day had arrived. We would be spending a weekend with fifteen LGBTQ people in the serene

Texas countryside singing worship songs, reading Scripture, and reflecting on God's place in our lives. I remember watching Karen walking up the sidewalk from the terminal and thinking, "Wow." My heart quickened, but I was determined to keep my cool. We loaded her bag into the car and drove off in search of a place to eat lunch. The rest of the afternoon was spent getting everything ready for the retreat, and Karen was a trooper through all of it. She pitched in wherever she was needed and blended in with the group. I liked that about her. This woman could take care of herself, and she wasn't afraid of new surroundings.

Throughout the weekend, I watched as Karen focused her energy on caring for those who had registered for the retreat, engaging with all the guests, and trying to make individual time for each one. I noticed her giftedness as a spiritual director, as she led us through reflection and prayer over the weekend, adding greatly to the overall experience for us. As the weekend drew to a close, I was tired, but I didn't want it to end. I wasn't looking forward to dropping Karen off at the airport. When we finally got to the terminal, after a two-hour drive, and unloaded her bag, we lingered to say good-bye. She hugged me tight and whispered in my ear, "I want a closer friendship with you." I told her I'd like that, too. She smiled and walked away, waving one last time as she headed toward the ticket counter.

I was hopeful but also nervous. What if she simply wanted to be friends? I didn't want to make more of it than it really was, but the way she hugged me felt different. I texted her while she was still waiting for her flight. After that, not a day went by when we didn't text or talk on the phone.

One thing I love about Karen is her straightforwardness.

Sometimes she can be a little blunt, at least to someone who's been brought up in a culture of passive-aggression under the guise of "Southern gentility," but most of the time she balances saying or asking what she's thinking with appropriate timing and phrasing. Lucky for me, she didn't want to drag out this "talking every day" if there wasn't more to it. I'll never forget getting a text from her as I was walking out of a movie with some friends. We had been talking for about a month at that point.

> So, I am on my walk and feeling I need to send a follow up to our call. For my own peace of mind, I need clarity on whether our communication is just for friendship or if there is more interest there. I am interested in you but wasn't sure if I should say something because there are hurdles like geography, and also we don't know each other very well yet. But I am expending too much energy wondering about it. So, I just need to name it and have clarity so I can move forward. No worries if you are only interested in friendship.

She was interested in more! My heart commenced pounding. I couldn't keep from grinning. I texted her back immediately and told her, yes, I was interested in more with her, that I didn't know what that might look like, living as far apart as we did, but that I very much wanted to see what might happen. We worked out a schedule to visit each other once a month for an extended period of four or five days. The first visit was Karen returning to Dallas, which meant I started thinking up fun things to do, things she would enjoy while she was here. I bought flowers, put them in a glass vase, and looked forward to seeing her reaction when she got here.

While I knew we would want time to ourselves to really get to know each other, I felt overwhelming joy at the thought of introducing her to my friends. I just wanted everyone to meet her. So, I chose carefully, and planned to balance the time we would spend just the two of us with the time we would spend with friends. When I first considered dating Karen, I shared this with several of my closest friends, both affirming and non-affirming. The beauty of sharing with all of them was that while they didn't all agree on the relationship, they agreed on loving me. Some might say that love requires "speaking the truth," and yet I had no question about where they stood. We had a long history with lots of conversation about what we believed on lots of things.

It's only been through deep, ongoing relationship that I have felt free to go to those friends and reconsider something about my life that no longer fit with what I believed God wanted for me. That's why the first person I told about my desire to enter into a dating relationship with Karen was my friend and pastor, Pat Bills. I knew Pat would receive me and love me just the same, whatever I told him. As it turns out, Pat went to dinner with Karen and me on our very first date! Now, how many can say that about their pastor? We had a great time eating at Gloria's and watching the sun set over Lake Ray Hubbard. Afterward Karen and I sat for the longest time with our feet in the water, watching the ducks and the boats coming in from a day of skiing or fishing. We talked forever. About things that really matter.

Like what we were looking for out of this relationship and what was most important to us.

One of the most important things we discussed from the very beginning was that we not have a secretive relationship. Karen told me that her relationships in her twenties, before her many years of celibacy, had all been secretive, leading to dysfunction and pain. She wasn't willing to go back to that, and she was clear with me that she wouldn't compromise. Either our dating relationship would be transparent or we wouldn't continue to date. "I want us to be open and honest with our families and friends," Karen told me, staring straight into my eyes and not flinching. I knew I wanted that too. But I also realized it would require me to face my fears of coming out again, as fully affirming and being in a dating relationship with a woman. That was new for me. And scary. But as I looked into Karen's eyes, I could see how important it was to her, and I was glad. I knew it was the right thing to do. We agreed to tell our families and close friends, with the intention of making a more public announcement on social media if and when the relationship became serious. Of course, one of the first people I told was my dad.

Daddy was eighty-eight years old when I made the drive up to Wichita Falls to spend the weekend with him. He lives independently in the home I grew up in from the age of fourteen, watching a lot of reruns of old westerns like *Gunsmoke* and *Bonanza*, but he also meets friends for coffee or lunch, and ever since my mom died, he's gone to breakfast every Saturday morning with his friend Rob. Daddy keeps up with the news somewhat, and every Sunday morning he drives to church and goes to eat lunch with friends.

I couldn't see my dad turning away from me. But still, I was anxious about how he would respond. Over the years I've talked with both of my parents about things I was learning about my sexuality, allowing for some rich conversation that helped all of us better understand what we thought we knew about being gay. In the last several years, my dad and I have continued those conversations by ourselves, just the two of us. Those talks made this one easier, but it didn't completely take the edge off.

After supper, I sat down on the couch that was closest to Daddy's recliner and told him I needed to talk to him about something. We turned the TV off, and he raised his chair up to listen.

"Daddy," I started, "do you remember me telling you a while back that I had come to see same-sex relationships differently – about how I no longer felt that two people of the same sex entering into a faithful, monogamous marriage was wrong? Do you remember that?"

"I know you've always been good to people who are married like that," he answered. We reminisced about couples he remembered, friends of mine he had met. We talked about books I had read and conversations I had had with people I trusted to help me understand Scripture. I reassured him that, ultimately, my change in perspective had come about through study of Scripture and that I still held Scripture in highest regard and had every intention of living a faithful life of service to God. Then I swallowed hard and took the plunge.

"Daddy, I met somebody."

I paused, but only for a second, before I launched into telling him about Karen. I told him where she grew up and where she'd gone to school and what kind of work she did.

"She loves God more than she loves me," I said, tearing up a bit. "I couldn't care for anybody who didn't put God first."

"I know that, Sally," Daddy said softly. He had a serious look on his face. I've come to know it as his "I'm listening intently" expression.

"Daddy, I don't know at this point where our relationship might lead, but I'm really tired of living by myself," I admitted. "I've lived by myself since I was twenty-two years old."

"I know you have," he said, tearing up now himself. "You know, I never really understood how hard that was until your mama died. Sometimes I still get so lonesome. I'm so sorry you've had to do that, and I didn't understand."

We both cried at that point. But I moved from where I was sitting on the couch and bent down on one knee on the floor in front of him and took both of his hands in mine.

Through tears, I went on, "Daddy, I need to know that you will be okay with me dating this woman. I don't want to do anything that would cause you to worry about me, or to be disappointed in me. What you and Mama think of me is what matters most to me. I don't want anything to change between us."

He reached over and handed me a tissue from the box on the table beside his chair.

"Don't you worry about that," Daddy said quickly. "I just don't want you to be alone anymore. That's all I care about. I know you, and I know you'll be faithful to God, no matter what. And your mama would tell you the same."

I wiped the tears from my face.

"Do you hear?" Daddy said. "Do you hear?" has always been one of Daddy's responses when he doesn't quite know what to say. But this time I heard it in the manner of loving reassurance that he intended.

We hugged and wiped our noses with more tissue.

"I think we need ice cream," I said. "Blue Bell. With chocolate syrup."

One of the things that many LGBTQ people miss out on is the opportunity to actually date someone. We don't get to learn about dating relationships as adolescents in the same way as those who are heterosexual do. When we're teenagers, we're busy trying to figure out what these feelings mean and keeping our sexuality a secret, especially those who grow up in conservative communities. That takes a tremendous amount of energy in itself. Instead of first dates and giddy and awkward conversations with parents, siblings, or peers about budding romantic interests, we're keeping our feelings secret. That can stunt relational maturity that is normally achieved by practicing healthy dating while we are still young like our heterosexual peers.

When LGBTQ adolescents or young adults are barred by their communities and families from pursuing a loving, committed relationship, many lose hope. Not uncommonly, LGBTQ people turn to poor substitutes to fill the longing to love and be loved by another. They begin to believe it's all a "lost cause," so why bother trying for anything better. Promiscuity or substance abuse can be the result of living without hope – the hope of building a home and family with someone, the hope of loving and cherishing another until death do us part.

One of the delights of dating Karen has been a transparent relationship with all the normal practices and rituals of courtship. It has felt amazing to date someone in a way that is completely natural for the very first time in my life. Instead of hiding our relationship, or our mutual affection for one another, we have been able to walk this journey openly. Neither of us had ever fully experienced that before. It has been fun introducing each other to friends and going on double dates.

The first time I visited Karen at her home in Durham, North Carolina, we had a lovely candlelight dinner with her dear friends, Lauren and Will. They fixed pasta and salad, and we brought a bottle of wine and chocolates. Karen had already told me so much about her friends that I felt as though I knew them already, but as we talked over dinner, and lingered over dessert afterward, I came to love them too. The best part of the evening, though, was rolling back the carpet, turning on the big band music, and having Will and Lauren teach us swing dance moves.

Dating has also opened up new worlds for me. Early in our relationship, Karen asked me to go hiking. She loves to hike and take long walks in nature. I was the student who drove across campus to my classes rather than walk, and my laziness has only worsened with age. So, when Karen asked me to go on an adventure with her at Eno River State Park, my mouth opened and the words, "Well, sure!" came out excitedly, but on the inside, I wasn't so sure at all. Karen packed sandwiches and chips in her CamelBak pack and filled two water bottles for us, and into the woods of North Carolina we went. Once we got onto the trail, and we could see the river surging below us, I found myself in a state of awe – awe at the beauty of nature around me, awe at the newness of this relationship that could so move me out of my comfort zone, and awe at the beauty of this woman walking ahead of me.

It was on one of those long walks that I realized I could spend the rest of my life with this woman. For on long walks we talked. And I learned more of the depths of Karen's intellect, her wisdom, her goodness, her knowledge of Scripture, her heart for God and for people, and I came to love every part of her. She is the person I want to make a home with. The one I know who will challenge me yet love me for who I am. The person I am proud to be with, for who she is and who we are together. Karen is the one I want to faithfully commit to for the rest of my life, and in that commitment, demonstrate the unfailing love of God.

I've been taught all my life that marriage is a covenant, a promise between two people, to share in every part of each other's life, good and bad. I was taught that marriage is forever. I was raised with strong convictions against divorce, which I still hold; therefore I take the thought of committing to someone for life very seriously. Marriage is kinship, becoming a family unit. God has breathed that longing into human beings from the beginning of time.

The decision to pursue marriage does not come lightly. It means lifelong commitment to each other's good. It means learning to put the other's needs above one's own. It means submitting to one another. It means we share everything. That won't always come easily. But marriage is getting up every morning and choosing, by God's grace, to love selflessly. Or, as the poet Wendell Berry writes about his wife, as he glances up at her on an ordinary day, noticing her beauty afresh: "Once more I am blessed, choosing again what I chose before."[1]

Part 4

Inviting the Church to Make a Difference

Just as a body, though one, has many parts, but all its many parts form one body, so it is with Christ. For we were all baptized by one Spirit so as to form one body — whether Jews or Gentiles, slave or free — and we were all given the one Spirit to drink. Even so the body is not made up of one part but of many.

Now if the foot should say, "Because I am not a hand, I do not belong to the body," it would not for that reason stop being part of the body. And if the ear should say, "Because I am not an eye, I do not belong to the body," it would not for that reason stop being part of the body. . . .

The eye cannot say to the hand, "I don't need you!" And the head cannot say to the feet, "I don't need you!" On the contrary, those parts of the body that seem to be weaker are indispensable, and the parts that we think are less honorable we treat with special honor. . . . If one part suffers, every part suffers with it; if one part is honored, every part rejoices with it.

(1 Cor. 12:12–26)

12

Loving the Samaritan

Pat Boone was our tribe's celebrity when I was growing up. The popular singer of the 1950s and '60s had very tangible roots in the Church of Christ in Tennessee, so he was definitely one of us. In the 1950s, Boone attended Lipscomb University in Nashville for two years, a college affiliated with Churches of Christ, before transferring to the University of North Texas. While in Texas, he preached at area congregations, but when his music career began to take off, he moved to New York City. With two gold records out in 1955, he stood in front of the congregation at the Manhattan Church of Christ and led them in a cappella singing every Sunday.[1] By the time I was born in 1961, Pat Boone was a household name in America, and folks in Churches of Christ were thrilled. Because he was one of us.

But I remember when the rumors about him started.

"You know, he's led singing at Abilene Christian University before – homecoming chapel, I think it was," one of my mom's friends told us as we were standing around talking in the pews after church one Sunday night. "We were there, and I remember he was so handsome. He had on a bright blue blazer, but he wore white shoes, right up there on the stage in Moody Coliseum. Everybody knows you don't wear white after Labor Day."

I was in elementary school, and while I didn't have full appreciation for who Pat Boone was, I knew that he had made a guest appearance on *The Beverly Hillbillies*. That was more than enough star power for me.

My mom's friend continued, "Well, Betty, you know he's just gone off the deep end. Left the church. Got involved with some charismatic group where they raise their hands during worship services. Somebody even said they spoke in tongues."

She and my mom just stood there, looking at each other, shaking their heads.

"Why, you know he won't ever be invited back to ACU, that's for sure," the friend said. "It's such a shame. He was so talented and all. Could have done a lot of good for the church."

Pat Boone had "gone off the deep end," I heard people say with a tone of sadness and disappointment. "He's all into that Pentecostal stuff now," they said. "He's no longer one of us."

What actually happened is that Boone's beliefs shifted from Church of Christ teaching on the present-day activity and power of the Holy Spirit, and he reported having the experience of speaking in tongues. He made television appearances with charismatic TV evangelists like Oral Roberts. All of this created quite a rift between Boone and Churches of Christ nationwide. Pat and his wife, Shirley, were disfellowshipped from the Inglewood Church of Christ, where they were members, in 1971, but Boone went on to serve as an elder for the Church on the Way, "a 'Spirit-filled' congregation in the Los Angeles-area community of Van Nuys."[2]

I was just a child when I heard those negative comments about Pat Boone, and I'm relating these conversations as best as I can remember. He wasn't the only one I saw shunned. People in my church at home had been expelled for various offenses. If we didn't live strictly by the guidelines of the church, which were taken from our interpretation of Scripture, we risked getting disfellowshipped. We would no longer belong.

In my humanness, I don't have the capability to know a person's heart fully and to decide when removal from community might actually be beneficial both to them and to the church. Admittedly, my experience is limited, but what this action has shown me over my lifetime is that it has never brought anyone to repentance. Removal – rejection – from the body has only served to create greater negative emotions, particularly shame and fear, not just for the person disfellowshipped but for all of us sitting in the pews, wondering who will be next.

The truth is, we too often expel or disfellowship people who are still devout followers of Christ. A person may not have done anything truly sinful. Instead, we wrongly judge others based on our own personal biases. Social scientific studies on disgust reveal that something we perceive to be different, that goes against our group norms, can elicit feelings of aversion and an effort to purge the "contamination" from our midst.[3]

The response of disgust can be helpful when applied to contaminants in a food source, for instance. But when this socially conditioned response is applied to people, it becomes problematic. We end up making moral judgments based on feelings instead of reason. The phenomenon of "moral dumbfounding" is when we feel something is morally wrong, but when asked why, we have difficulty explaining a rationale.[4] We then conjure up reasons to justify the feelings of disgust rather than recognizing that the reaction can come from a place of bias. But there is a better way: "Embrace [of others] must be *deep*. Further, it must be *prior to any judgements, moral or otherwise, we make of persons*. Only then will the fundamental humanity of the person be protected from the psychology of disgust and dehumanization . . . the will to embrace must be the communal starting point. No discussion of hospitality or church discipline can commence until the will to embrace the dignity of others is firmly in place."[5]

I am troubled by some churches' quick impulse to disfellowship others, especially without taking the time to reflect that they may not be seeing the situation clearly. If God retains the right to "have mercy on whom [he will] have mercy" (Rom. 9:15), then who am I, a mere human, to assume who is in and who is out?

When I was in the second grade, my Sunday school teacher, Amy Walker, gave us each a children's book that told a Bible story. We were supposed to take the book home and learn the story so that we could retell it to the class on the Sunday we were assigned. My book was the story of the good Samaritan in Luke 10:30–37. I remember standing in front of the small classroom filled with seven- and eight-year-old boys in suits and ties with their hair slicked back, and little girls in dresses with white socks that turned down to their ankles and patent leather shoes. At seven, this was my insight into the story: I was supposed to live like the good Samaritan, and that meant if I came upon anyone who needed my help, I was to be willing to go out of my way to help.

As a Christian, I wasn't supposed to be like the religious leaders of the day who walked right on by without lifting a finger to help the man who had been beaten and left by the road to die. This was my understanding of the story for a long, long time. It wasn't an incorrect understanding of the parable. In fact, that Christians are to help people in need was an excellent message for second graders to hear. It's just that there is far more to the story. And it wasn't until my adult years that I came to see the deeper message for me from the parable of the good Samaritan.

I was particularly inspired by the insights of Don McLaughlin, who spoke at our very first CenterPeace conference in Abilene in 2009. Don is the longtime lead minister of North Atlanta Church of Christ in Atlanta, Georgia. In his final keynote address on Saturday morning of the conference, he brought to life the literary context of the good Samaritan story.

> On one occasion an expert in the law stood up to test Jesus. "Teacher," he asked, "what must I do to inherit eternal life?"
>
> "What is written in the Law?" he replied. "How do you read it?"
>
> He answered, "'Love the Lord your God with all your heart and with all your soul and with all your strength and with all your mind'; and, 'Love your neighbor as yourself.'"

> "You have answered correctly," Jesus replied. "Do this and you will live."
>
> But he wanted to justify himself, so he asked Jesus, "And who is my neighbor?" (Luke 10:25–29).

So Jesus answers the man's question, "Who is my neighbor?" by telling the parable of the good Samaritan. I've always thought of the neighbor as the man who was beaten, robbed, and left lying in the ditch. The bad guys in the story are the religious leaders who walk by doing nothing to help, and the good guy is the Samaritan. Of course, my tendency is to identify myself as the hero of the story; after all, I like helping people. But what if I'm really the guy in the ditch? It changes everything, because Jews did not associate with Samaritans. Samaritans were despised as unclean gentiles. To simply eat from the dish or drink from the cup of a Samaritan made a Jew ceremonially unclean.

That's why the story is so scandalous. Jesus is making the hero in the story out to be a Samaritan.

It is easy to put ourselves in the place of the helper. But how much more vulnerable and disconcerting to receive help from someone we dislike or even despise. The story asks us to imagine someone who disgusts us as the hero of the story. The one that the Jews believed engaged in false worship is portrayed as the very one who does God's will by showing compassion. The Samaritan is willing to go out of his comfort zone, to do what inconveniences him. The "unclean" person is the one who helps the injured man by the side of the road. Neither the priest nor the Levite was willing to do this, even though their lives were supposedly centered on serving God. They are the ones we would expect to show kindness and compassion. But instead it's the "despised Samaritan" who ends up doing the right thing.

So, what is Jesus really trying to teach us with this story? When Jesus asks the expert in the law who the neighbor in the story is, the expert must answer, "the one who showed mercy." But to a Jew, to acknowledge that the Samaritan is the neighbor, the neighbor we are called to love as ourselves, this teaching was radical. The story invites us to ask today, who is my neighbor? Who do I consider "unclean" or feel an aversion toward? It means I'm supposed to love the last person on Earth I would expect to love. The person I've been taught to stay away from, for fear of "contaminating" my reputation, my morality, or other people's opinions of me.

The Samaritan today is the person I've been told isn't one of us, perhaps because of something they believe or don't believe. Someone who doesn't belong. The person I've been taught to believe is evil, or just wrong. This is the neighbor I'm called to love as myself. And when I look closely enough at their life, I may see something totally different than what I expected. In God's eyes, the Samaritan was doing the will of God, following the great commandment to love his neighbor. Yet, he was mislabeled and misconstrued by the very ones who claimed God was on their side.

I can't help but think of this parable when I remember encounters that I've had with people who hold different perspectives from me, people I've been taught to view as "other" and to avoid, lest I become like them. It's ironic, but the people who have disagreed with me, holding more progressive views, have often shown me more kindness than those who shared the same traditionalist views I once had on same-sex relationships. I went into those encounters with judgment perceiving myself to be in the right, when really, I was the guy in the ditch being offered help. It was the person I had been told was so wrong who showed me kindness. This hasn't always been the case, but it's happened enough to remind me that fellowship in Christ goes far beyond our self-constructed walls.

When I moved back to Abilene to begin teaching communication classes at Abilene Christian University, I started attending the Sojourners Bible class on Sunday mornings at Highland Church. I had a lot of friends who went to that class, and I enjoyed the fellowship. I came to love that time, not just for the coffee and chocolate donuts from AM Donuts but also because of the teacher, Richard Beck. He was funny and personable and had an engaging teaching style that drew people into the lesson as though it were a conversation. Richard is incredibly insightful, a psychology professor at ACU with the brilliant mind of a true academician wrapped in the body of an eccentric old hippie. Upon first sight, I didn't quite know what to think of this man who wore jeans and a wrinkled shirt and had tattoos and bracelets all up his arms. His hair was long and stringy. But the more he talked, the more I listened. Because this man clearly loved the ways of Jesus.

That's what made it all the more troubling and confusing when I began hearing rumors about Richard. I kept hearing there was a professor on campus who was affirming of same-sex relationships. I was still a traditionalist in my theology at the time, and the news startled, even agitated, me. How in the world could we have someone teaching at my alma mater who was supportive of same-sex relationships? I couldn't understand this. When I discovered from some of my students that the professor in question was Richard, I wasn't sure how to respond.

The students, on the other hand, had nothing but good things to say about Richard. They loved him. I paid attention to that and realized it made no sense for me to make judgments about someone over something I'd never heard him talk about, without even so much as having a conversation with him. I was convinced that if he did indeed believe same-sex relationships were okay, that he was wrong, but I was also wrong for thinking harshly of someone I hadn't bothered to get to know more personally.

One Sunday morning after Sojourners class, I invited Richard to get coffee sometime during the week and talk. We got out our calendars, found a convenient time for both of us, and chatted a bit before walking into the Sunday morning service at Highland. I fretted all week about what we would talk about, and what I was going to say about his views on sexuality. I had not yet read any of the books that laid out an affirming view of same-sex relationships, for fear that my own views might be challenged. So I felt more than a little apprehensive when I arrived at Starbucks for our meeting later in the week.

I don't remember all the specifics of what we talked about, other than the ministry work I had begun doing with CenterPeace. He was nothing but kind and genuine and supportive of my desire to bring dialogue about faith and sexuality to the forefront of the church. On top of that, he was funny and down to earth. As we talked, my judgment melted away. I was reminded of Richard's heart that I had come to see during his Sunday morning Bible class. Somehow it didn't seem important anymore to investigate his beliefs on sexuality, and I didn't end up confronting him directly about it. Instead, I was reminded of all the ways his love of Jesus was clearly demonstrated in his life. I couldn't ignore that evidence.

Richard taught the radical hospitality of Jesus in a way I'd never heard before, talking about "The Little Way" of Saint Therese of Lisieux and Dorothy Day's work among the poor in New York City. There was a humility about him. I began to consider all the ways in which I'd observed Richard living a Christlike life. Not only did he teach the Sojourners class and care well for his students at ACU, but he also led a weekly Bible study at a nearby prison. Richard didn't fit the stereotypes I had of someone who approved of same-sex relationships. He hadn't gone off the deep end. He was a true follower of Jesus and lived that out in tangible ways.

Over time I came to know Richard even better, and his example of what it means to be a Christian had a significant impact on me. He ended up being one of the regular teachers at Freedom Fellowship when I was playing drums in the praise band there. Wearing dark blue farmer's overalls and a shirt with the sleeves rolled to three-quarters of his arm, exposing his tattooed forearm, Richard blended in with the crowd at Freedom. Here was a guy who lived in the world of academia, a guy who could write on the deepest intellectual levels, and yet every week I was astounded by the way he connected with the audience at Freedom. Many of our friends at this church have learning challenges, and haven't finished high school, let alone gone to college. But Richard seemed as comfortable at Freedom as he did in academic circles. When people in the audience called out comments or questions spontaneously, Richard affirmed and incorporated their answers into his lesson. He never seemed put off when he was interrupted, as I would have been if I had been teaching.

Presenting deep theological principles with simplicity, Richard taught in ways that allowed everyone to take home an important lesson about God. Sometimes he turned a Johnny Cash song into a lesson, playing the song and having us sing along. Other times he used a simple visual, like the medieval painting of a group of monks worshiping at the feet of Jesus on a cross. The artist of that picture suffered from leprosy and lived among a colony of lepers, so he painted lesions on all the worshipers. But the most touching aspect of the painting was the artist's placement of lesions on the body of Jesus. I have a copy of that picture, and it reminds me of the truth that Jesus knows and experienced all my maladies, that he knows what it's like to be me. Richard reminded those of us at Freedom that we have a Savior who knows what it's like to be us – to be poor, to be hungry, to be cast aside.

I also learned from watching Richard that my understanding of a devout Christian had been too narrow. I saw the Holy Spirit working in and through this man, who held different views on an issue I had considered nonnegotiable. And if God was with him, who was I to judge my brother?

In the spring semester of my first year teaching at ACU, shortly before I shared my story in chapel, Tony Campolo came to campus. Dr. Tony Campolo is an internationally known evangelical pastor and professor emeritus of sociology at Eastern University in Philadelphia. Tony was there to speak at a weekend retreat on service learning. Since I was part of the initiative to incorporate more service learning projects into our course offerings, I attended the retreat. And because I wanted to talk to him privately, I finagled my way into being Tony's ride from the event back to his hotel. I was nervously preparing for my upcoming chapel presentation, the first time I would be sharing my story publicly, and the thought of being able to talk with Tony comforted me.

I don't recall how I first heard of Tony. Probably, a preacher had retold one of his compelling stories for a sermon. But I do remember how much I anticipated finally getting to hear him in person. When the time came and he began speaking, I had to chuckle to myself, for he reminded me of the old comedian Don Rickles, whose voice was brusque and loud with a bit of a Brooklyn brogue. The major difference being that Tony wasn't about put-downs for a laugh. He was one of the most powerful preachers I'd ever heard. And his stories were one of a kind. He shared his ministry reaching out to downtrodden prostitutes, including children who had been trapped in the sex-trafficking industry.

After the Saturday evening session, I got my car to take Tony back to his hotel. A bit nervous, anticipating what I wanted to talk to him about, I pulled up to the auditorium door in my silver Toyota Solaris and picked him up. It was a cold January night, so I turned on the heat as we drove off campus. We made small talk until we turned onto the main road to the freeway, and then I launched into my request.

"Dr. Campolo, I've got something I'd like to ask you to pray about," I began, keeping my eyes on the road for more than one reason. "You see, I'm on the faculty here at the university, and I'm going to share my story in chapel. I'm going to tell them about how I am attracted to women. I'll also tell them that I don't think that's how God wants me to live, but it's still really scary."

We eased onto the freeway that looped around Abilene. Tony sat quietly, listening, looking straight ahead.

"I'm scared to death about how people will respond – my students and fellow faculty members who don't know yet," I told him, gripping the steering wheel tightly with both hands. "But I know this is something God is calling me to. We've got to talk about this in Christian settings."

"That's very brave," he said, glancing over at me. "I think you're right about needing to talk about this among Christians."

I instantly felt relieved.

"But you know, Sally, I've worked with probably two hundred students over the years who have told me they're gay. They've just agonized over it, tried everything they were told to do to change, and they haven't changed. And then they agonize more, thinking, what's the matter with me that I didn't choose this, and I can't even get rid of it!"

I knew the feeling.

"I just don't know," Tony continued, shaking his head, still looking at the road in front of us. "I just don't know if this is something that can be changed about a person. I know some people say that, but I've known too many who couldn't. They are good, faithful Christians. I just don't think you can change."

"But I think it's possible for my attractions to change," I declared. Signaling to take our exit off the freeway, I put my foot on the brake gently and eased onto the service road. I was telling Tony what I believed at the time. Later I would come to realize he was right. But that night, driving Tony back to his hotel, I still held on to hope.

We arrived at Tony's hotel, and I pulled up under the portico by the main door to let him out.

"May I pray for you right now?" Tony asked.

I told him, "I'd love that."

Tony took both of my hands and bowed his head. His strong voice softened as he began praying for me. He prayed for courage, peace, receptive hearts, and understanding. He patted my hands affectionately, thanked me for the ride, and got out of my car.

Wow, I thought, on the way back, even Tony Campolo has been hoodwinked. He doesn't think sexual orientation can change. How can someone who is such an extraordinary preacher not believe that "all things are possible with God"? I was disappointed. I had been moved by his stories that night, but Tony clearly didn't think as I did on same-sex sexuality. Yet, he prayed for me just as I asked before he left. And he seemed to accept me exactly where I was.

A year later, Tony was back in Abilene, speaking at a citywide gathering of churches in Moody Coliseum one Sunday morning. It was during the winter and quite chilly, so I grabbed my coat on the way out the door. By the time I arrived, the service had already begun. I stood on the floor of the coliseum trying to find a seat because the place was packed. I could see Tony sitting on the rostrum along with several other men who were leading the service. Quickly I found a seat, just as Tony was beginning to speak. Again, I was moved by this man's passion and wit, his stories of radical hospitality for people we tend to overlook, his compassion and tenderness yoked with strength in defense of the oppressed. Tony reminded me a lot of my picture of Jesus. I hung on every word.

After the service, I made my way down to the front. It was a long way, and it took me a while to weave through the crowd on the floor of the coliseum. By the time I got to the front, people had cleared out and Tony came over to where I was standing. Before I could remind him of who I was, he greeted me.

"Hey, I saw you come in back there! You came in late!" he said, laughing.

"I know, but I made it just in time," I said. I was about to tell Tony about having shared my story in this same coliseum just months after he and I talked, but before I could begin, he started talking.

"Say, how did it go? You know, when you talked in chapel? Did you tell your story?" he asked, eyes glistening, as if he couldn't wait to hear the answer.

I couldn't believe he even remembered who I was, let alone our fifteen-minute conversation while driving across town to his hotel. But he did remember. Not just me, but what we talked about and what he had prayed for me. Quickly I told him it had gone well and that there had been an overwhelmingly positive response.

"Oh, that's great!" Tony said, "I'm so happy for that. And I'm proud of you. Blessings on you." He gave me a warm hug and a wide smile. I'm sure my smile back at him was just as big. I couldn't believe this man who preaches literally all over the globe, who has taught thousands of students and meets new people constantly, remembered someone who gave him a ride to his hotel one night. But he did. And his response – his joy – was sincere. In fact, Tony's response to me was far more receptive, despite our different beliefs on same-sex sexuality, than the response of many who shared my traditionalist beliefs at the time. Our difference didn't keep Tony from receiving me and celebrating the doors that God opened through that chapel talk.

Several years later, Tony would publicly announce that he believes God affirms same-sex relationships – a conclusion he drew only after much prayer, study, and reflection. His shift in viewpoint was denounced by many in his community, leading him to express how alone he felt being pushed away from people who had once been his colleagues and friends.[6]

I've never forgotten those brief encounters with Tony Campolo, nor the fact that he had spent time listening to and praying for two hundred gay people during his time as a professor at Eastern. At that time in my life, I didn't know many Christian leaders who had had that much contact with gay people. That made an impression on me. That, and his prayer for me, asking God for courage, peace, receptive hearts, and understanding. At the time, I thought only the first two of those requests were for me. But in time it was my own heart that became more receptive and understanding.

13

Saving the Next Generation

Last year when I came across the headline "Report Projects 35 Million Youth to Leave Christianity by 2050," I did a double take.[1] This can't be right, I thought. But I shouldn't have been surprised. It's all we've been hearing for over a decade now, about how the younger generations are leaving church. Or they don't even consider church membership in the first place because of negative perceptions of Christianity. I remember having a wake-up call after reading *UnChristian* back in 2007. When three thousand unchurched young people ages sixteen to twenty-nine were asked their opinion of Christians, a common response was that Christians are judgmental and hypocritical. One number that stood out to me was how many young people, those in the church (80 percent) and those who are not (91 percent), perceived Christians as "antihomosexual."[2]

The thought of younger generations not being a part of the church deeply saddens me. It troubles me to think of them going through life without the guidance, nurturing, and encouragement that I have received from being part of a faith community. And yet, the surveys and polls indicate that more young people are leaving the church – leaving Christianity – than ever before. To stick our heads in the sand and lie to ourselves that we tried all we could, or that our culture was just too strong an influence, or that our kids are simply rebellious, would be to take the easy way out. But if we believe in a God with whom all things are possible, then we must not give up.

When Mark passed away in 1994, hardly anybody at our church knew he had died of AIDS. Mark had been clarinet section leader in band during the spring of my freshman year of high school, and he was the best clarinet player I'd ever known personally. Mark had made all-state band almost every year in high school on two different instruments, clarinet and alto saxophone. He was a gifted musician. He went to college, and three years later I joined him, sitting in the band hall with him at Abilene Christian University. We also had a history class together that year, so we ended up studying together at Pizza Hut or Mr. G's.

I knew Mark was gay from what other kids in school said about him. But that never kept me from hanging out with him and being his friend. He got sick in the early '90s, and I heard through the grapevine that he was HIV positive. Several months before he died, Mark came home to live with his parents, Jake and Blanche. But they never said a word about Mark being gay, or what caused his death. Not even when my mom looked at Blanche through tears and told her there was nothing that was too big for them to bear together. Not being able to express their feelings had to have been agonizing for Mark and his parents.

There was no discussion of same-sex sexuality in our churches, except for condemnation.

I wish I could say things have changed in twenty-five years. In some ways they have. But many LGBTQ young people still feel trapped in a church culture of silence and shame. In the summer of 2013, Toby called me. My memoir, *Loves God, Likes Girls*, had just come out, and she had read it and wanted to talk. Toby grew up in the same church that Mark did. And like us, she had played in the high school band. I remember watching her a few years earlier on the field during my thirtieth high school reunion, scheduled around the most important football game of the year, the game against our long-standing crosstown rival. As I sat in the stands with my old classmates, it made me smile to hear the band playing the traditional tunes we had played back in the day, like "March Grandioso," our fight song, and marching off the field to the classic "Young Lions."

I was especially proud of the drum major that night, because I had known Toby all her life from a distance. Her father and two aunts had gone to high school with me, and their family went to the church my parents attended. Whenever I visited my parents' church, I would see the cutest little brown-eyed girl named Toby sitting with her grandparents. Now she was a senior in high school and drum major of the band. It thrilled me to watch her direct on the field. At the time, I didn't yet know she was struggling to make sense of her attraction to girls.

When Toby contacted me, my mom was ill in the hospital, so I asked if we could talk there. We found a couple of comfy waiting room chairs in a new section of the hospital and sat for the next couple of hours talking. Toby had ended up going to

Vanderbilt on a full music scholarship on trombone. The more she talked and the more I observed the intensity with which this young twenty-something listened and engaged me in conversation, the more I realized how keenly intelligent Toby was, and emotionally mature well beyond her years. Yet, as we sat there talking, I knew I was talking to a deeply troubled soul.

Toby was deeply troubled in the same ways I had been at her age. She was attracted to women, and yet she was a faithful, committed Christian. She had gone to church with her parents, but more often with her grandparents. Her grandmother had been one of the church secretaries, and her grandfather was a deacon. Her life experiences, while different in many ways, mirrored mine. Here was someone who could have been my child, who went to the same schools, lived in the same town that I grew up in, and marched in a band for four years of high school, just like I did. And now she was wrestling with her faith and sexuality, just as Mark and I had at her age.

As I sat there listening to her, I remembered a conversation I had with a new elder at Toby's church in the early years of CenterPeace. When I told him about the work I do, he said, "It's really nice what you are doing, but we don't have anyone here like that at our church." I had hoped that since that time the church had made changes. But it was clear that Toby was having to cope with so much pain on her own. A chill went up my spine as I came to the realization that three decades later Toby was having to endure the same shame and secrecy that Mark and I had endured. In the same town, the same school, the same church.

Toby continued to share her heart with me, telling me how she was encountering similar barriers in churches in Nashville, where she had moved to attend Vanderbilt University. Someone had given her a list of churches in the area to try. When she finally found one that felt at home, she soon became disheartened. Toby had joined the college group, and the minister told them they could ask anything and the group would take time to talk about it. So, Toby wrote "homosexuality" on a notecard and put it in the basket. Every Wednesday night she went, hoping and praying this would be the night the college minister would help the group talk through the topic, but they never did. So Toby left.

"Wow," I said. "That's unbelievable."

"Yeah, it was superdisappointing, like the main thing that I've been wrestling with, and even when you ask to study with somebody, it's ignored," Toby confided. "I have so many questions, but it's like nobody wants to talk about this in church. They either tell you 'the Bible is very clear,' and that's that, or they get all embarrassed and avoid it like the plague."

"I know, Toby. It was the same when I was your age."

That conversation with Toby was a turning point for me. Looking into her eyes, observing her sweet countenance, hearing the love she still has for God, I could not bear the thought that the church might let her slip away. Here it was 2013, and the same challenges I had faced thirty years earlier were *still* happening. It was disillusioning. Ever since that conversation, I have felt an increasing urgency to reach our young people. While Toby has managed to persist in staying connected to church, finally finding an affirming congregation in Disciples of Christ, too many of both LGBTQ and straight young people I have met over the last fifteen years of my work with CenterPeace no longer attend church.

The coffee shop I'd suggested we meet at was closed when I arrived. I buttoned up my coat against the cold and texted Cori, telling her we'd have to find another place. She texted back, and we agreed to meet at a different shop around the corner. As I walked to the new destination, I wondered what Cori would share with me. I'd never met her before. We'd only texted a few times after her therapist recommended CenterPeace as a resource to address her concerns about sexual identity. She was all of eighteen.

When I arrived, I looked around the shop for someone her age, guessing at what she might look like. I found her sitting at a table near the coffee counter, with a toboggan on, her long blondish-brown hair cascading down her back. She wore glasses, and when she looked up and saw me, her face broke into a smile. Cori already had something to drink, so I got in line to order a hazelnut latte while she saved our table. It felt good to be in such a warm and cozy place, even if it was particularly noisy and crowded.

Our table was off in a corner, so I hoped Cori would feel comfortable talking to me there. I couldn't imagine having to ask a stranger to meet me, to talk about my sexuality, out in public like this – anywhere, quite frankly – when I was only eighteen. I was thirty-five before I told anyone about my attraction to women, and that was my therapist, David. I'm always moved by the courage of young people who have talked to me over the years, about the conflict they experience in trying to resolve their faith with their sexuality. I am glad the conversation has opened up more since I was their age, so they don't have to wait as long as I did to get help.

When I got back to the table with my coffee, I took off my coat and placed it on the back of my chair. We made small talk for a while, then Cori started to open up about her life, her realization that she was attracted to girls, and the fear and shame she had experienced ever since. She said she had been able to talk to her parents, but the rest of her family didn't know she was gay. She mentioned how difficult it was going to be to talk to her grandparents. She told me about what it was like to grow up in a missionary family, living in a foreign country when she was a little girl. Now they were back in the States, and her family attended a church I knew well.

It was obvious to me from the beginning of our conversation that Cori had no desire to leave her faith by the wayside. She told me about a recent family vacation where they all read one of Peter's letters from the New Testament and discussed it together. Undoubtedly, this young woman came from a devout Christian family, and she valued her faith. But she was deeply troubled by this part of herself she didn't choose, the attractions she couldn't make go away, no matter how fervently she prayed.

We talked for a couple of hours that day. But then I lost contact with Cori for a while. I found out later that she had been hospitalized for severe depression, to the point of seriously attempting to take her own life. That is where the story might have ended. But it didn't. By the grace of God, family support, and ultimately, Cori's spirit of determination, she is still with us. More than that, she is thriving.

Two years after her hospitalization, Cori is now an integral part of a leadership team I'm involved with that is planting an open and affirming Church of Christ in Dallas. Cori is the youngest member of our team, but without a doubt, one of the most faithful Christian souls I know. She loves Scripture and knows the stories of Jesus and all the faithful people in the Old and New Testaments that we become acquainted with in Sunday school. She has a heart of compassion for others. Cori is a leader among her generation and a light into the future. When I think of her, I have hope that we can reach the next generation.

The church plant pastor, John Ogren, and other leaders on the team have made a point of both supporting Cori and affirming her gifts. Sometimes that means meeting with her one-on-one to help her work through something she is going through. And sometimes it means asking her to serve in ways in which she is gifted. Each week Cori begins our time together with an icebreaker reflection question. It may be as simple as what was your favorite birthday celebration, but hearing each other's life experiences always enriches our time together.

This summer the fledgling church has been meeting in a park on Sunday nights. After singing worship songs with Brad and Nathaniel on guitar and Megan on the djembe, we listen to each other's concerns and pray. We share the Lord's Supper together. And we read a passage of Scripture aloud and discuss it. More than once I have been deeply moved by Cori's insights. Recently at one of our gatherings, she talked about how Luke 21 had taken on new significance to her, as she read it in light of LGBTQ people. It was the passage where Jesus tells the disciples they will experience persecution, insults, and rejection from friends and family but that he would be with them.

Cori explained, "This passage speaks to me because I know a lot of LGBTQ people who could relate to being hated, myself included. Rejected by people close to you. Knowing Jesus is with us during that – that's just really comforting to me."

I can't imagine what it would be like to not have Cori with us. I can't imagine what would have happened to Cori had her parents believed that the best thing to do for her spiritually was to cast her out of their home. Instead, they continued loving, nurturing, and caring for all her needs as a teenager. What would have happened if Cori no longer had Christian community, missed out on songs about the "overwhelming, never-ending, reckless love of God," and didn't have people love her just as she is, who listen and pray with her? What would happen if she had no place to read through the book of Luke every week, or people to read it with, to talk about how the stories of Jesus apply to us today.

We have lost too many opportunities to nurture and disciple young people. At a time when their hearts are so open and shapeable, we sabotage any desire they may have to do kingdom work, by continuing to believe lies that drive them away. And not just our LGBTQ children but our straight children as well, for they have hearts for their LGBTQ friends, and they can spot our inconsistencies a mile away. God is inviting us to spiritually nurture and disciple our LGBTQ young people, to encourage them in the gifts God has given them to serve the church.

Two and a half years ago, I invited four or five LGBTQ Christian friends to dinner at my home. We talked about the need for Christian fellowship among the LGBTQ community. We talked about the friends we each had who had become so discouraged from serving, from using their gifts, from just going to church, that they had stopped. Each of us committed to invite a friend to the next dinner in one month. Anyone was welcome. Anyone. We agreed to have everyone contribute something for our meals and to rotate who hosted the dinner. We also decided that there would be no proselytizing. Our monthly gatherings would be nothing but sharing dinner and conversation together. No strings attached, no expectations, no "six months you're good and then the hammer drops" – just dinner. Creative souls that we are, we decided to name our gathering "Just Dinner."

The next month we had ten people. The month after that we had nearly twenty, and the size of the group kept growing over the next several months. We peaked at a little over forty one summer night when ice cream was all we had for dinner! Like Jesus modeled for us, we simply gather people around a table, and it's amazing what can happen. Like when Jenn showed up.

When I first moved to Dallas, I asked around for a good veterinarian for my dog, Chester. Chester had seizures and would need his medication monitored, plus I was going to have to board him during my frequent travels for work. I wanted to find a place that would take good care of him, because he wasn't a pup anymore. Some friends at church recommended Four Paws Animal Hospital. After several months of dropping Chester off to board, one of the staff members whom I knew to be gay asked me, "What kind of work do you do that you have to be gone so much?"

Continuing to fill out the paperwork for Chester, I answered, "Well, I direct a nonprofit, and part of that job is conducting workshops at different churches all over to help them be more welcoming to LGBTQ people."

"Really," she said, more as a statement than as a question.

"Yeah, it's hard to believe, but a lot has changed in churches. People are realizing we haven't responded well."

"No kidding," she said and rolled her eyes.

I handed her the paperwork, and she put an invoice in front of me to sign.

"I know firsthand that we haven't responded well because I was a gay kid who grew up in church. That's why I started this nonprofit, to help churches better understand and not drive LGBTQ people away."

"Yep," she chuckled knowingly, entering my credit card information on her computer screen. Under her breath where only the two of us could hear, she said, "Damn sure drove me away."

I would later learn that Jenn had grown up in the church but left in her teens, vowing never to return, after suffering unspeakable pain at the hands of a youth pastor.

While I was waiting for one of the kennel workers to bring Chester up from the back of the building, Jenn asked me more about what I present when I work with the churches that invite me to speak.

"It depends a lot on where people are in their thinking and experience with someone who is LGBTQ," I told her. "If they've never had a conversation with someone who they knew was LGBTQ," I went on, "then I have to start with the very basics, helping them understand that a lot of the myths they've bought into about us simply aren't true. If we can just tear down the lies that cause otherwise good people to believe they're justified in condemning, that's a big step."

Jenn sat in her swivel chair, arms folded, staring at me for a while.

"That's really cool," she said finally. "I'm glad you're doing that."

Pretty soon one of the vet techs brought Chester out, and we left. But from that day on, I never went into Four Paws without talking with Jenn. Sometimes we shared what movies had come out that we wanted to see, as she's a movie buff like I am. Mostly, though, on the days I dropped Chester off to board, our conversation started with Jenn asking me where I was going and whom I'd be talking to on this trip. Whenever I came home and stopped by to pick up Chester, Jenn always wanted to know how "things" went.

I had known Jenn for about three years when I invited her to Just Dinner. By then Chester had died and I had adopted a new puppy, a dapple dachshund I named Rudy. I happened to be picking up Rudy from Four Paws on a day that we were scheduled to have Just Dinner at my house. Jenn was tending to my paperwork, so in the course of our conversation I mentioned having dinner with LGBTQ friends at my house and invited her to come. I wasn't sure she would. But a few hours later, after everyone else had arrived, the doorbell rang. It was Jenn, standing on my porch holding a jar of pickles.

"Here," she said, handing me the pickles. "I came, now I can go home!"

Jenn turned around as if she were going to start walking back to her car, then looked back at me with a grin.

"Get in here!" I said, reaching my arms out to hug her as she stepped into my house.

My dining room table and the table in the kitchen were both full, but people got up and made room for Jenn. It wasn't long before I heard raucous laughter coming from the kitchen. Jenn's humor had kicked in, and she had the table in stitches. After dinner we wandered into my living room for dessert and coffee, sharing transparently about our lives with one another. Today we have Just Dinner groups meeting not only in Dallas but also in Fort Worth and Austin, Texas; Birmingham, Alabama; Edmond, Oklahoma; Nashville, Tennessee; and Victoria, British Columbia, Canada. Of course, the Canadians had to be different and do "Just Brunch"!

Reaching out to the next generation can be as simple and profound as hosting dinner. The gift of the church, when at its best, is its ability to create a communal sense of belonging — with no strings attached. Caring community can be healing. This is especially true when people have had hard and painful experiences with the church. Only the balm of Gilead can heal those kinds of wounds. Some wounds will take a long, long time to heal. And I believe God has called upon us to initiate the process and be patient. To love and befriend with no expectations. Over a bowl of chili and cornbread. Over Mexican stack. Over ice cream out on the deck on a hot summer night. During a meal at our homes. This is where we experience the very tangible love of Christ, without even needing to utter his name aloud, because we most certainly know and experience him in our midst.

For every story like Mark's, Toby's, Cori's, and Jenn's, there are thousands more. Over the years I've met so many young people who have been exuberant in the expression of their faith. They've wanted to go into ministry, vocational missions, teaching, social work, seeing all of these as an outgrowth of their love for God and how they would "be Jesus" to the world. And yet, in the process of growing up and discovering that their sexuality was different in some way than that of their peers, they have not felt free to pursue those callings. Silence and shaming have turned our young people away, making them feel they have no home in the church. As Don McLaughlin, lead pastor of the North Atlanta Church in Atlanta says, we have created "spiritual orphans." I long for young LGBTQ people to grow up being spiritually nurtured and affirmed in their gifts, for them to feel connected to the rich heritage of Christianity.

What if LGBTQ people never had to worry about not being wanted by their families or by their churches? What if the energy they expend trying to figure out what their feelings mean, and the energy they use trying to keep anyone from finding out about their sexuality, was directed toward deepening their relationship with God? I grieve for all that the church has lost and continues to lose because we have not adequately met our LGBTQ youth where they are and in the ways they need. God is inviting the church to learn, to sit down with the LGBTQ people in our midst, and to ask what it's been like to walk in those shoes. God is inviting the church to encourage our LGBTQ young people to develop the gifts God has given them.

May we pass down to the next generation a picture of God that looks like Jesus, a God who is loving above all and compassionate, so that young people will become so intrigued with the life of Christ that they give themselves over to him in every way. May we pass down Scripture as a love letter, full of stories of how God relates to us and guides us. May the songs we sing – songs that teach us the gospel, long before we know what the words mean – be engraved into the hearts of LGBTQ people, so that in those most discouraging moments of life they might remember and draw comfort from what we believe. I hope that future generations return to our pews and fill our worship services with voices that raise the rafters, making it hard to find a seat again on a Sunday morning.

14

Why I Stay

Recently, someone asked me why I stay in the church or remain a Christian, given the way LGBTQ people have been treated. But even though the question has flickered through my mind before, I've never seriously thought of leaving. The truth is, I can't imagine my life without Christ or the spiritual community that raised me. A significant portion of my earliest, formative memories – memories that provide a picture of my past and give me identity – revolves around my experience in the Church of Christ. To this day, I could re-create a map of the church building of the congregation I attended for the first seventeen years of my life. I was as familiar with that building as I was with the house I grew up in. And the interactions I had in that space, as well as the lessons I heard, and the lyrics we sang, have dramatically shaped who I am.

Simply knowing I come from a heritage of people who tried earnestly (albeit sometimes too earnestly) to read Scripture anew and discern patterns for worship and for living that were pleasing to God inspires me to continue doing the same. Even with all our overemphasis on being right in the Church of

Christ, of using Scripture to proof-text a point, and all the other ways our humanness got the better of us, I still cherish, in our very best moments, a deep and abiding desire to be pleasing to God. That's why I stay.

I come from a tradition within the Restoration Movement that, at its heart, wants to return to the ways of Jesus and the practices of the early church. That principle beckons us to reexamine ourselves, reform ourselves, and seek to grow more into the likeness of Christ.

One of the great blessings of my life has been being a part of churches that have not just allowed me to grow but have encouraged me to grow in my understanding of the Christian faith. I have been privileged to sit at the feet of men and women who have not only taught me well the stories of Jesus but by their words and example have called me to explore for myself what Christianity is all about.

I have been most fortunate to be exposed to teaching that emphasized learning, knowing that would lead to changes, in the ways we worship, in the ways we interpret Scripture, in the ways we see and value each other. Not only has the Restoration Movement of my tribe provided a basis for constant reexamination, but the autonomy of Churches of Christ has permitted congregations to continually reform, still upholding our love and respect for Scripture and faith traditions while being open to greater understanding of God's will for us.

Some in my tribe have incorporated instruments into their assemblies. We've incorporated women's voices into worship and leadership roles that were unheard of thirty years ago. Why? Because, as our forefathers envisioned, we are willing to continue to go back to the text and discern matters communally, as the first-century church in the book of Acts did upon finding that "it seemed good to the Holy Spirit and to us." I am so thankful to have been a part of churches that were willing to expand their views of God while returning to what Jesus called the two greatest commands: Love God and love your neighbor.

I have stayed in the church because I got to sit at the feet of Christian preachers like Rick Atchley, a minister whose sermons, in my college and young adult years, fed my soul and planted another layer of foundation for my faith. I recall a lesson he taught on a Wednesday night in the late 1980s centered on the woman in Mark 5, who had been bleeding for twelve years. Over the years I have come to increasingly cherish this story. I relate to the menstruating woman, not because of her physical malady but because she was different in a way that she didn't choose and couldn't alter, leaving her unclean by her community's standards. Since the law required menstruating women to be isolated, she would have been mostly alone for twelve years. She risked everything to come to Jesus. And Jesus did the unthinkable at the time; he acknowledged someone considered unclean. He didn't turn her away, nor was he in any hurry to be rid of her.

Over the years, other preachers like Mike Cope, Randy Harris, Don McLaughlin, Landon Saunders, and Pat Bills have inspired me, opening up Scripture for me in ways that I had not yet been exposed to, helping me to see more clearly the love of God and to grow in my understanding of what the life of a Christ follower looks like. Their preaching and my participation in important community gatherings within my tribe, like Abilene Christian Summit, the Pepperdine Lectures (Harbor), Lipscomb University's Summer Celebration, and the Zoe Conferences, offered me still more opportunities to grow in my understanding of God. These voices taught me ways of hospitality, belonging, and unconditional love. They also opened my world to still more Christian ministers and theologians, like N. T. Wright, Walter Brueggemann, Eugene Peterson, Brian McLaren, Brennan Manning, and Henri Nouwen, further enriching my understanding of Christianity.

Within my world of Churches of Christ, I found space to breathe. Paradoxically, the spiritual heritage that sometimes digs in its heels, insisting it is right without deeper reflection and is suspicious of what is new, also recognizes the need to continually go back to the basics of the Christian faith, to the beginning and the simple loving ways of Jesus and the church. It is my tribe that taught me that Jesus created a place of belonging for the unclean woman, bleeding in isolation, when no one else would welcome her. And that is why I stay.

When I was in the second grade, my parents gave me a Bible for Christmas. It was a small, black leather King James Version, and I carried that Bible to Sunday school and Wednesday night Bible classes every week until I was fourteen years old. I underlined verses I was encouraged to memorize and highlighted passages by shading them with pencil, just as my mom had done in her Bible that was falling apart. But for my fourteenth birthday I wanted a different Bible, because I wanted to understand the Scriptures better.

The summer before my fourteenth birthday, we had a gospel meeting at my church with a preacher from St. Louis named Stanley Shipp. Every night of the meeting Stanley preached, and on Saturday he spent the day with our youth group. He had a heart for young people. Back in St. Louis, Stanley worked with young adults, preparing them to go into urban areas, working in teams to plant churches. I would later meet friends in college who ended up joining those teams, planting churches in Miami, Florida, and in Connecticut.

The main thing I remember about Stanley's meeting with my youth group was the Bible he was using. It didn't have all the "thees" and "thous" that my Bible had. It sounded more contemporary, like the way people talked now, and I liked that. It was easier to understand. When Stanley read a passage from his Bible, it was dynamic and inspiring. Once, when we were all sitting in a circle with Stanley, I was sitting close enough to glance over and see that his Bible had extra stuff on the sides and at the bottom of the pages. I wondered what that was about, so when we took a break, I talked to him about it.

"This," he told me, holding his Bible up, "is a *Harper Study Bible*, Revised Standard Version." Stanley was sitting across from me in one of the metal folding chairs set up for our meeting that day. His eyes got big as he explained all the study aids it contained and the full concordance at the back. When he held it up, I could see how thick it was. I was particularly impressed with the information at the beginning of each book, which related when a book might have been written and who wrote it. I went home that day and told my mom I wanted a *Harper Study Bible* for my fourteenth birthday.

Scripture has always been a source of comfort and guidance for my life. In times of sorrow, the Psalms have been a resting place for me. Realizing the full range of emotion expressed throughout the Psalms, I have been able to wrestle with my own difficult emotions, anger toward God, doubt, pain from the loss of friends, and the death of loved ones. Sometimes I've written a verse on a notecard or a sticky note to carry in my pocket, pulling it out from time to time throughout the day as a source of encouragement.

In times of deep depression, when I've felt most alone carrying burdens only God knew, I've gone back to Psalm 34:18 to remind myself that

> The LORD is close to the brokenhearted
>   and saves those who are crushed in spirit.

When I first felt my family rising out of the pit of secrecy and shame that we had been in for the first three decades of my life, again it was a psalm that spoke most clearly to my heart.

> If the LORD had not been on our side—
>   let Israel say—
> if the LORD had not been on our side
>   when people attacked us,
> they would have swallowed us alive
>   when their anger flared against us;
> the flood would have engulfed us,
>   the torrent would have swept over us,
> the raging waters would have swept us away.

Praise be to the LORD,
  who has not let us be torn by their teeth.
We have escaped like a bird
  from the fowler's snare;
the snare has been broken,
  and we have escaped.
Our help is in the name of the LORD,
  the maker of heaven and earth. (Ps. 124)

I'm still moved to tears when we sing "Had It Not Been the Lord," a song based on this psalm. I now lovingly call this my family's song.

Shortly after I began to dream of sharing my story more publicly, another psalm became an anthem for my life.

I cry aloud to the LORD;
  I lift up my voice to the LORD for mercy.
I pour out before him my complaint;
  before him I tell my trouble.
When my spirit grows faint within me,
  it is you who watch over my way.
In the path where I walk,
  people have hidden a snare for me.
Look and see, there is no one at my right hand;
  no one is concerned for me.
I have no refuge;
  no one cares for my life.
I cry to you, LORD;

I say, "You are my refuge,
    my portion in the land of the living."
Listen to my cry,
    for I am in desperate need;
rescue me from those who pursue me,
    for they are too strong for me.
Set me free from my prison,
    that I may praise your name.
Then the righteous will gather about me
    because of your goodness to me. (Ps. 142)

I have also found solace and guidance in the Gospels. The stories of Jesus have inspired me more over the years than I ever thought possible – the stories of his interactions with Zacchaeus, the woman at the well, the woman caught in adultery, the woman who washed his feet with her tears at the house of Simon the Pharisee, and most of all, the woman who bled for twelve years. It's the self-sacrificial love that I see in Jesus that compels me to hold fast to my faith. It's his love and grace for me that call and enable me to forgive those who have hurt me, to turn the other cheek, to love my neighbor as myself – even my enemy. Jesus challenges me to be a better person than I ever would be left on my own.

It was the church that first taught me to love the Scriptures, in whose pages I first met and still find Jesus. It was my tribe, however fallible, that first taught me those comforting psalms. And it is my heritage that continues to encourage me to look to the Scriptures for wisdom. That is why I stay.

Growing up, I was taught to call people at church "Brother and Sister so-and-so" rather than "Mr. and Mrs." Anyone we went to church with was considered family. But it wasn't limited to our own congregation. Everyone who was a member of the Church of Christ was considered family. I might not know them personally, but if I visited another congregation, anywhere in the world, we were instantly connected by our common belief in Jesus. And if we stood around and visited long enough after church, we would most often find that we were connected by association. It's sort of a joke in Churches of Christ that we all know each other, and although this is not as true as it once was, we are still a fairly close network. In the course of conversation, it doesn't take long to find mutual friends and acquaintances, wherever you go.

There's something powerful about that – having friends in common with people all over the place. I can't imagine living without the global community of siblings in Christ. Being connected to people provides a sense of belonging. Perhaps my experience is more rare than I realize, but this is something I love about the Christian community. I love the feeling of being part of something bigger than myself. When I was little, my mom would always tell me, "Now, Sally, if you ever need help, if you're out somewhere and you need help with anything, you find a church, and somebody there will help you."

I experienced the truth of this in Lubbock, Texas, during graduate school, when I was conducting research for my master's thesis. Just as I drove into town I had a flat tire on the car I was driving, a pale yellow 1970 Oldsmobile Vista Cruiser station wagon with wood-grain paneling and a moon roof, the car we had purchased brand-new when I was in the third grade, the car I had driven all my friends around in during high school and college and now was on its last legs. Driving down one of the main thoroughfares of town, I looked up and saw the sign Broadway Church of Christ and pulled into the parking lot. I followed the signs to the office, and just as soon as I opened the door, I recognized a friend from college sitting at one of the desks. We both threw our hands up in the air and shrieked, alarming everyone else in the office. But not for long, because they understood. Someone came out and helped me change the tire.

When I moved back to Abilene, I was embraced by the Highland Church of Christ in powerful ways. I felt the support of my elders in the creation of CenterPeace and the ministry work I was doing, but I also felt connected to friends who cared for me and loved me through all kinds of circumstances. When I moved to Dallas, I became involved with the Highland Oaks Church of Christ. Thanks to minister Pat Bills, I got to know the staff and was embraced by a small group. Again, there were warm greetings and hugs every Sunday morning, extending into the week with phone calls and texts and invitations to meals.

And when I was diagnosed with breast cancer, my Highland Oaks family rallied around me. I never went to a chemo infusion alone. Sharon McIlroy and Kim Westbrook took turns picking me up every three weeks for the four months of the hardest chemo, and stayed all day with me. One day there were so many visitors that the nurses moved us to a private room! People brought food and left protein shakes, and once the executive minister, Becky Burroughs, came just to clean out the refrigerator. And when I couldn't walk from the swelling in my legs caused by the chemo, Pat came on Sunday mornings and rolled a wheelchair up to my front door and took me to church.

My church family was also there when my dog, Chester, died. I loved Chester like he was my baby. Not too long before I started chemo, Chester, thirteen years old, became seriously ill. A part of me knew that he was suffering and I couldn't stand that, but another part of me couldn't imagine taking Chester's life. That evening I texted friends from church, Tom and Kristie, because I knew they loved dogs and would understand. It was late, but they both immediately responded. In talking to them it became clear that because Chester was suffering, it would be best to take him to the veterinary clinic that night.

I was devastated. I adored this dog. He had been with me through some of the most difficult circumstances of my adult life. I loved the way he held one tennis ball in his mouth while pushing another with his nose, wanting me to play fetch. The way he would climb up on my lap and lick the tears off my face when I cried. I couldn't stand to lose him.

Chester and I hadn't been at the emergency clinic for very long when the door opened, and there stood Tom and Kristie. The doctor examined Chester and recommended going ahead and putting him out of misery. Tom and Kristie sat with me the whole time. Then they came back with me to my house, even though it was well after midnight. They were in no hurry. Their only concern was me at that moment.

I know not all churches are alike. And I have to acknowledge that in some congregations I wouldn't feel particularly at home, or welcome at all. For my LGBTQ Christian siblings who have struggled in vain to find churches they can belong in and experience authentic community in, this saddens me. But I remain hopeful. I have personally witnessed churches and individual believers reflecting the loving family of God. The body of Christ, at its best, is a place of belonging like no other. And that's why I stay.

The last time my mother was in the hospital, the night her cardiologist had come by one last time to tell us there was nothing more he could do for her congestive heart failure, Mama found comfort in an old hymn. The nurse had given her something to help her sleep around nine o'clock, and she slept soundly until around two in the morning. I was sleeping restlessly in a chair that folded out into a twin-size bed, right beside her bed. The room was dark except for narrow strands of light from outside, splashing through the blinds on the window and onto the wall that faced Mama's hospital bed. Hearing Mama stir, I woke up and patted her hand.

"Sally, can you see that? Oh my, it's the most beautiful place I've ever seen!" Mama exclaimed.

"No, Mama, I can't see it. What do you see?" I asked, figuring she was having a hallucination, common with urinary tract infections among elderly women, or from the medication to help her sleep. But she surely wasn't sleeping now. She continued staring straight ahead at the wall in front of her, pointing at times to the grandiose scene she was telling me about.

"Oh, Sally, I wish you could see it," Mama kept saying. "It's just beautiful."

Mama would try to describe the place to me, telling me it was prettier than any place we'd ever been. Lovelier than Yellowstone or any of the mountains in Colorado. More majestic than the Alps of Switzerland. She would tell me about the pastures full of wildflowers, lots of her favorite bluebonnets, and a calm stream rippling over rocks, down through the pasture. I continued to ask her what else she saw, but this was the scene she kept coming back to. I asked her where she was, and at first she didn't know. But as the vision wore on into the wee hours of the morning, it occurred to her where she was.

"Sally, I think this must be heaven. I've just never seen anything this beautiful before," Mama told me. "Oh, honey, you don't ever have to be afraid to come here. It's a wonderful place."

I don't know how many times Mama told me that no one should be afraid to go there. But I knew that as she often had, she was helping herself not to be afraid by telling me it was okay.

Every now and then she would begin to sing, "How beautiful heaven must be," and then immediately I would come in on the familiar bass part, echoing, "must be." She laughed, and so did I. I could hear her smile as she continued to sing. For the rest of the night I held her hand and listened as she told me about the picture of heaven she had been given. I kept asking her if she saw anyone she recognized besides Jesus. She said she didn't, but forever the elementary school teacher, she was overjoyed at how many children she saw running about in the pasture. Then she would start to sing again, repeating the chorus over and over until at last, about five thirty in the morning, she finally drifted off to sleep.

Many would say my mother's vision was simply an effect of the medication, and perhaps it was. But I prefer to believe it was her faith, which had embedded this place called heaven in her mind nearly ninety years earlier, and when it was time, she was able to see it. It brought my mother comfort in her last days on this earth, and it brought me comfort, too.

A big part of the reason I first chose to believe was because my mother believed. My grandparents believed, and all my family, and all the people who were central to my life believed. I felt as though I belonged to something bigger than myself. Feeling connected to my mother and all those who have passed from this life whom I still love and long to see spurs my faith. I cannot prove to you that this part of the gospel story is true, that we'll all be raised from the dead one day to live in eternity together. I have no way to prove that. But I want to believe it's true. I want to carry my mother's faith with me, melded into what is now my own. And that's why I stay.

Resources

CenterPeace, a §501(c)(3) nonprofit organization founded by Sally Gary, has been providing resources for LGBTQ Christians, families, and churches on faith and sexuality since 2006. We provide a place to belong for LGBTQ people, including faith-nurturing retreats and community online and in person. We offer workshops for churches, universities, and other organizations, both private and public, to provide insight regarding matters that affect LGBTQ people. CenterPeace is also a supportive resource for parents of LGBTQ children. For more information, visit our website at centerpeace.net.

And follow us on these social media platforms:

- Facebook – facebook.com/centerpeaceinc
- Twitter – @centerpeaceinc
- Instagram – @centerpeaceinc

Recommended Further Reading

Beck, Richard. *Stranger God: Meeting Jesus in Disguise.* Minneapolis: Fortress, 2017.

———. *Unclean: Meditations on Purity, Hospitality, and Mortality.* Eugene, OR: Cascade, 2011.

Brownson, James. *Bible, Gender, and Sexuality: Reframing the Church's Debate on Same-Sex Relationships.* Grand Rapids: Eerdmans, 2013.

Cacioppo, John T., and William Patrick. *Loneliness: Human Nature and the Need for Social Connection.* New York: Norton, 2008.

Cron, Ian. *Chasing Francis.* Grand Rapids: Zondervan, 2013.

Davis, Ellen F., and Richard B. Hays, eds. *The Art of Reading Scripture.* Grand Rapids: Eerdmans, 2003.

DeFranza, Megan. *Sex Differences in Christian Theology: Male, Female, and Intersex in the Image of God.* Grand Rapids: Eerdmans, 2015.

Enns, Peter. *How the Bible Actually Works.* San Francisco: HarperOne, 2019.

———. *The Sin of Certainty.* San Francisco: HarperOne, 2016.

Keen, Karen. *The Bible and Sexuality.* Durham, NC: Contemplatio Publishing, 2020.

———. *Scripture, Ethics, and the Possibility of Same-Sex Relationships.* Grand Rapids: Eerdmans, 2018.

Kinnaman, David, and Gabe Lyons. *UnChristian: What a New Generation Really Thinks about Christianity . . . and Why It Matters.* Grand Rapids: Baker Books, 2007.

Lee, Justin. *Torn: Rescuing the Gospel from the Gays-vs.-Christians Debate.* Nashville: Jericho Books, 2012.

Manning, Brennan. *Abba's Child: The Cry of the Heart for Intimate Belonging.* Colorado Springs: NavPress, 2015.

———. *The Ragamuffin Gospel.* Colorado Springs: Multnomah, 2005.

Marin, Andrew. *Love Is an Orientation: Elevating the Conversation with the Gay Community.* Downers Grove, IL: InterVarsity Press, 2009.

———. *Us versus Us: The Untold Story of Religion and the LGBT Community.* Colorado Springs: NavPress, 2016.

Martin, Colby. *Unclobber: Rethinking Our Misuse of the Bible on Homosexuality.* Louisville: Westminster John Knox, 2016.

McDonald, Greg, and Lynn McDonald. *Embracing the Journey: A Christian Parent's Blueprint to Loving Your LGBTQ Child.* New York: Howard Books, 2019.

McLaren, Brian. *A New Kind of Christianity.* San Francisco: HarperOne, 2010.

McLaren, Brian, and Tony Campolo. *Adventures in Missing the Point: How the Culture-Controlled Church Neutered the Gospel.* Grand Rapids: Zondervan, 2003.

McLaughlin, Don. *Love First: Ending Hate before It's Too Late.* Abilene, TX: Leafwood, 2017.

Noll, Mark A. *The Civil War as a Theological Crisis.* Chapel Hill: University of North Carolina Press, 2006.

Stanglin, Keith D. *The Letter and Spirit of Biblical Interpretation.* Grand Rapids: Baker Books, 2018.

Venema, Dennis R., and Scot McKnight. *Adam and the Genome: Reading Scripture after Genetic Science.* Grand Rapids: Brazos, 2017.

Vines, Matthew. *God and the Gay Christian.* Colorado Springs: Convergent Books, 2014.

Volf, Miroslav. *Exclusion and Embrace: A Theological Exploration of*

Identity, Otherness, and Reconciliation. Revised and updated. Nashville: Abingdon, 2019.

Wingfield, Mark. *Why Churches Need to Talk about Sexuality: Lessons Learned from Hard Conversations about Sex, Gender, Identity, and the Bible.* Minneapolis: Fortress, 2019.

Notes

Prologue

1. Dennis Jernigan, "Make Me More Free," *This Is My Destiny* (Here to Him Music, 1999).

2. Sally Gary, *Loves God, Likes Girls: A Memoir* (Abilene, TX: Leafwood, 2013), 238.

Chapter 1

1. "At Calvary" was written by William R. Newell in 1895. Public Domain. Lyrics retrieved from https://hymnary.org/text/years_i_spent_in_vanity_and_pride.

Chapter 2

1. Richard Beck, *Unclean: Meditations on Purity, Hospitality, and Mortality* (Cambridge: Lutterworth, 2012), 121. Beck has written and spoken extensively about the radical hospitality of Jesus on his popular blog, *Experimental Theology*, and in two of his best-selling books, *Unclean* and *Stranger God.*

2. Christine Pohl, *Making Room: Recovering Hospitality as a Christian Tradition* (Grand Rapids: Eerdmans, 1999), 13.

3. This is part of the legal standard for determining negligence.

Chapter 6

1. This is the translation from the 1984 NIV, which was in use at the time I met with my colleague. The NIV was updated in 2011, and the rendering of 1 Cor. 6:9 is now "men who have sex with men." The updated NIV obscures what Martin Luther's translation of "boy molester" more accurately captured. Namely, in antiquity, same-sex activity was more often between men and *boys*, not primarily men and men.

2. For more on this, see the Forge Online, "Has 'Homosexual' Always Been in the Bible?" *United Methodist Insight*, October 14, 2019, https://um-insight.net/perspectives/has-"homosexual"-always-been-in-the-bible/.

Chapter 11

1. Wendell Berry, "The Wild Rose," in *New Collected Poems* (Berkeley, CA: Counterpoint, 2012), 314.

Chapter 12

1. Bobby Ross Jr., "Disfellowshipped Decades Ago, Pat Boone Insists He 'Never Left' Church of Christ," *Christian Chronicle*, September 24, 2017, https://christianchronicle.org/excommunicated-decades-ago-pat-boone-insists-never-left-church-christ/.

2. Ross, "Disfellowshipped."

3. Richard Beck, *Unclean: Meditations on Purity, Hospitality, and Mortality* (Cambridge: Lutterworth, 2012).

4. Beck, *Unclean*, 63.

5. Beck, *Unclean*, 139.

6. "Tony Campolo Says He Feels Alone Following Changed Stance on Homosexuality," *Premier Christian News*, October 26, 2016, https://premierchristian.news/en/news/article/tony-campolo-says-he-feels-alone-following-changed-stance-on-homosexuality.

Chapter 13

1. Samuel Smith, "Report Projects 35 Million Youth to Leave Christianity by 2050," *Christian Post*, September 24, 2019, https://www.christianpost.com/news/report-projects-35-million-youth-to-leave-christianity

-by-2050-greg-stier-responds.html. The Barna Group predicts a decline in church membership among younger generations and an upswing in the number of adults reporting no religious affiliation: "Church Dropouts Have Risen to 64% – but What about Those Who Stay?" September 4, 2019, https://www.barna.com/research/resilient-disciples/.

2. David Kinnaman and Gabe Lyons, *UnChristian: What a New Generation Thinks about Christianity . . . and Why It Matters* (Grand Rapids: Baker Books, 2007).